NEW
ENGLAND DIESELS

by
DAVE ALBERT
and
GEORGE F. MELVIN

There are **4000** numbered
copies of this first edition
of
NEW ENGLAND DIESELS
of which this is
Copy Number   1992

Cartography by Three-D's, Inc.,
    Omaha, Nebraska.
Typesetting by Tyler Type Service,
    Lincoln, Nebraska.
Graphics by Omaha Graphics, Inc.,
    Omaha, Nebraska.
Printing by Interstate Book Manufacturing, Inc.,
    Kansas City, Missouri.

END PAPERS —
Front: Boston & Maine FT's #4223 AB and 4221 AB roll an eastbound freight through Hastings, Massachusetts on April 23, 1953. *(Dave Albert Collection)*
Back: Maine Central #710 leads Train 163 eastbound for Portland at Miles Pond, Vermont on a frosty April day in 1955. In the distance are the snow-covered peaks of Mt. Washington and the Presidential Range. *(Jim Shaughnessy)*

GEORGE R. COCKLE and ASSOCIATES
POST OFFICE BOX 1224, Downtown Station, OMAHA, NEBRASKA 68101

NEW ENGLAND DIESELS

This book is dedicated to the professional railroader whose cooperation and helpfulness make our hobby more rewarding.

NEW ENGLAND DIESELS

3

FOREWORD

The task of compiling the contents of this book began in the spring of 1974. During countless "bull sessions", which are as much a part of our hobby as the taking of photographs, the talks would tend to drift back to the early years of the diesel; discussing the colorful paint schemes, operations and variety of trains, all the while lamenting on how the whole spectrum of railroading in New England had changed. "Why not do a book on the subject?", was the question asked. And, "Why not?" was the reply.

In this volume, we bring forth the works of both the noted and littleknown photographers; some of whose material is being published for the first time. We can be thankful for this group of dedicated men who had the patience and skill and took the time and effort to record for all time, the scenes on the following pages.

Since the trend in recent years is to nostalgia, the longing to go back in time, then let these pages of time take you back to the beginning of a new era for the railroads of New England; the coming of the diesel and the four decades that have since followed.

Waterville, Maine
1976

DAVE ALBERT
GEORGE MELVIN

ACKNOWLEDGEMENTS

We would like to express our sincerest gratitude and appreciation to the following people, without whose interest, generous help and photographic contributions, this book would not have been possible: Friend, advisor and publisher George R. Cockle, another new found friend and publisher G. B. Davies, Russ Munroe, Jr., Arch McDonnell for his unique cover painting, Dr. Philip R. Hastings, Jim Shaughnessy, Roger P. Cook, Scott Hartley, Paul Westin for his technical assistance and research, Bradley Peters and Edward Galvin of the Maine Central Railroad's Public Relations Office, Richard Sprague - Vice President of Public Relations for the Bangor & Aroostook Railroad, Dwight A. Smith, J. Emmons Lancaster, 470 Railroad Club, Frank DiFalco, Herman Shaner, Ronald N. Johnson, Henry Preble, Donald S. Robinson, John Egan, Wayne D. Allen, Howard Kirkpatrick, Joseph Ryan, Al Lawrence of the New Haven Railroad Technical Information Association, Dick Symmes of the Walker Transportation Collection - Beverly Historical Society, Stanley M. Hauck, Norton D. Clark, George Pitarys, Robert Baker, Sr. and Robert Baker, Jr., Wayne Duplisea, Jack Swanberg, Joseph R. Snopek, Alan Thomas, Jack Armstrong, Don Woodworth, Ken McDonald, Ed DeVito, Dan Foley, Robert Redden, Jerome Rosenfeld, Neil Richardson, Dave Engman, Bob Mohowski, Jay Potter, Harold K. Vollrath, Neil Shankweiler, Phil Faudi, Richard B. Gassett, Alco Historic Photos, Don Don Dover - EXTRA 2200 SOUTH and Edward A. Lewis.

TABLE OF CONTENTS

NEW ENGLAND DIESELS

The Story

New England.....Just the mention of this historic part of the United States brings images to mind. An independent spirit, strong ties with the past, Yankee ingenuity, and good old Downeast stubborness typify the will of the of this six-state region. These same characteristics will be found in an examination of the way that the railroads of the region undertook the eradication of the steam locomotive from their rails. New England found some of the diesel's earliest converts crossing paths with some of the last holdouts of steam. Indeed, diesels were replacing diesels at the same time that steam was making its last stand in the next valley!

• • ● • •

The year 1931 turned out to be the most prophetic year of all for the New Haven Railroad. The Depression was now firmly underway and efforts were being taken to cut costs in operations. Impressed by the sales pitch of the American Locomotive Company, the New Haven invited Alco to demonstrate their new 600 HP switching engine. After a trial period the New Haven was impressed enough by the little unit with the tall sloping hoods to purchase it and number it 0900. As the 0900 went about its tasks, crews were favorably impressed by the good visibility and the clean, relatively quiet operation of the "oil-electric" unit. The New Haven's management was undoubtedly just as impressed with the 0900's low operating costs and high rate of availability. The 0900 remained the only diesel in New England until 1934, when the Boston & Maine took delivery of a very similar Alco unit, the main difference being the replacement of the sloping hoods with straight sides.

The year 1935 brought another switch engine to the Boston & Maine, this one being a twin-engined center cab unit built by General Electric and powered by Ingersoll-Rand. This unit became Boston & Maine 1100. Much more noticeable than any previous diesels in the area, however, were the first passenger diesels. With the nation being dazzled by Burlington's "Pioneer Zephyr" in 1934, the idea of traveling by streamliner was too much to pass up for anybody with enough cash to buy a ticket. Boston & Maine and the New Haven both responded to the new idea by introducing streamliners of their own. The B & M, along with stepchild Maine Central, ordered a copy of the "Zephyr" from Budd and the Electro-Motive Corporation placing it in Boston to Bangor service as the "Flying Yankee". The New Haven's "Comet" was a curious-looking one-of-a-kind built by Goodyear-Zeppelin and powered by Westinghouse. Of the two, the "Flying Yankee" was the

more successful, both from an operational standpoint and from public acceptance. The Boston & Maine also acquired the first two diesel-powered railcars in 1935.

In 1936 the New Haven ordered ten switchers from General Electric. All ten had identical welded bodies but five had Ingersoll-Rand engines and the balance Cooper - Bessemer, with the provision of interchanging engine types if desired. These units were of road switcher configuration with a short hood housing the cooling system ahead of the cab. The Boston & Maine, influenced by its experience with the "Flying Yankee", ordered the first Electro-Motive switchers in New England, the 600 HP model SC, while jointly-owned (with Maine Central) Portland Terminal Company took delivery of three Alco HH—600's.

The only activity in 1937 was the New Haven taking delivery of the last of the units ordered in 1936, but 1938 found HH—600's going to the B & M, N H, and P T Co., while the B & M got more SC's from EMC. New York Central's Boston & Albany received its first diesels in 1939, and following experiences of neighboring roads, ordered Alco HH—600's. Alco introduced its new model 539 prime mover in 1939, and the N H and B & M followed the Maine Central in ordering 539-powered HH—660's, at 660 HP. Electro-Motive also introduced a new power plant in 1939, and the B & M quickly took delivery of three SW—1 switchers, the first in the region. As history has shown, the 1939 introduction of the model 567 engine was probably the single most significant development in all of dieselization. In these three diminutive SW—1's, the Boston & Maine brought the now familiar sound of the 567 to New England, a sound heard to this day throughout the six states.

In 1940 the New Haven reordered HH—660's to bring its fleet of diesel switchers to thirty-one. General Electric introduced its 44-ton centercab switcher in 1940 to comply with the 90,000 pound limit for one man operation, and the Boston & Maine again was the pioneer of a new model diesel in New England, buying four of the tiny units.

Past purchases of switch engines continued in the year 1941. Maine Central bought the first New England example of Alco's newly designed S—!, which had the HH—660's internal components rearranged in a low-hooded carbody. New Haven and Portland Terminal followed with purchases of their own S—1's. New York Central began buying S—1's in 1940 but it is not known if these units were initially assigned to the Boston & Albany. Later in the year, the Portland Terminal introduced the Alco S—2

NEW ENGLAND DIESELS

to New England. The S—2 offered 1000 HP through the turbocharging of the 539 engine in the S—1. Imagine.......... thirty-five years ago, Portland Terminal 1051 could be called "New England's most powerful diesel"! Central Vermont followed the P T by taking delivery of its first diesels, two S—2's. These were part of a three unit order, the first two coming in December 1941 and the third in January 1942. This turned out to be the C V's only purchase of diesels until 1951. Other diesel purchases in 1941 included B & M's reorder for SW—1's and the first B & M NW—2's, a 1000 HP switcher powered by a twelve cylinder model 567 engine. The B & M also received three more 44-ton GE's, while relative M E C received its first of that type. In several instances, the two roads bought similar type locomotives even bearing consecutive serial numbers, suggesting joint orders were placed. At this time, N H also became a 44-ton owner.

The real breakthrough of 1941 was still to come. Up to this time, every diesel in New Engalnd was a switcher type except for the two streamliners and the two B & M railcars. No diesel was in road service handling conventional freight or passenger runs. Following its pioneer spirit of 1931, the New Haven placed an order for the first road diesels in the region, and began taking delivery of ten Alco DL—109's in December 1941. Each DL—109 was powered by a pair of turbocharged model 539 six cylinder engines, yielding a total of 2000 HP. The units rode on two three-axle trucks, with the center axle being an unpowered idler axle to distribute weight and improve riding qualities. The DL—109 was intended as a passenger locomotive, having a boiler for train heat, but the New Haven used the units in a dual-service role....handling passenger runs outside the electrified zone in the day, and working freight at night. The units were not without "bugs", especially in the cooling systems, but subsequent orders of DL—109's bear out the fact that these problems were overcome. The New Haven was the seventh of seven railroads in the country to purchase the DL—109, but eventually purchased ten times more DL—109's than the next largest owner, the Southern Railway. Dressed in rich hunter green and yellow, the DL—109's made a fine sight speeding passengers to their destinations.

By 1942, World War II was well under way, resulting in military traffic coming to the rails. A side effect of the war was the War Production Board's decree that only General Motors could build road locomotives and only Alco and Baldwin could build switchers. How much this policy eventually hurt Alco and Baldwin will never really be known, but it put the two minority builders in an underdog position after the war, since efforts at the development of a new prime mover had to wait until the war's end. The B & M received the last EMD switchers to come to New England until the end of the war in the form of three NW—2's. The Central Vermont's third S—2 arrived and the New Haven reordered S—1's. The M E C and B & M each got one additional GE 44-tonner, the last to come to the region until 1945. The New Haven received the remaining units of the 1941 DL—109 order, and somehow got permission from the War Production Board for Alco to construct ten more DL—109's, and these began to arrive in July 1942.

The year 1943 brought EMD road diesels to the region in the shape of six A-B sets of FT freight diesels for the B & M. Each A-B set yeilded 2700 HP and unlike neighbor New Haven's DL—109's, the FT's had two axle trucks with no idlers, but were really two seperate locomotives connected with a drawbar. The handsome maroon and gold units were put in Mechanicville - Worchester - Boston - Portland freight service. These units were significant in that they were able to run through Hoosac Tunnel without assistance from the electric motors used to move

steam powered trains through the 4.75 mile bore. Other 1943 arrivals were the last of the N H 1942 DL—109 order, more S—1's and the first S—2's for the New Haven, and a single S—1 for the Portland Terminal.

In 1944, eighteen more A-B sets of FT's came to the B & M and the N H ordered twenty more DL—109's. The Boston & Maine received its first S—1's and S—2's from Alco, since SW—1's and NW—2's were not available. The New Haven also bought switchers in 1944, getting more S—1's and the remainder of all the S—2's that it would own.

Relaxation of tensions in 1945 saw only the New Haven and Boston & Maine with major commitments to dieselization. The Maine Central, Boston & Albany, Portland Terminal and Central Vermont owned only handfuls of switchers while the Bangor & Aroostook, Rutland, Grand Trunk and Canadian Pacific owned no diesels at all. The Bangor & Aroostook in particular had just made a large commitment to steam, building several modern servicing facilities for steam power. Their idea was to acquire good steam power displaced from the rosters of other roads by diesels. 1945 saw the B & M receiving its first passenger diesels, 2000 HP E—7's from EMD. The E—7 was similar in construction to the DL—109, riding on A-1-A trucks and having two prime movers. The New Haven got the last of its 1944 order of DL—109's and re-ordered 20 more, bringing its total ownership of this model to sixty. More switchers came in 1945; M E C and P T getting S—1's, B & M getting S—2's, and the N H and M E C acquiring more 44-tonners. Electric-powered shortline Aroostook Valley began diesel operations in 1945 with a pair of 44-tonners, the first shortline in New England to purchase that model.

Alco freight locomotives appeared on New England rails in 1946 in the form of the 241-powered "Black Maria" test units. After extensive trials on the New Haven both in freight and passenger service, the units went north for a stint on the Bangor & Aroostook, and thus became the first diesels to operate on that road. Although never duplicated, with the 244 engine winning out over the 241 version, the test units were at least partially responsible for the New Haven's order for FA—1's and FB—1's in 1947. On the other hand, the B A R, always a staunch Alco customer in steam, was dismayed with the test units' shortcomings (two of the three units became inoperable while testing on the B A R) and never bought an Alco diesel new. Perhaps the "Black Maria" units were responsible for this as new EMD diesels started arriving in 1947. Purchases in 1946 included NW—2's and SW—1's for the B & M, an S—2 for the P T, M E C got a 44-tonner and its first E—7's, while the B & M got the balance of its 1945 order of E—7's. Boston & Maine brought the first F—2's, a sort of updated FT, to the region, getting 18 cabs and 3 booster units. Fifteen of these F—2's were bought to work with single FT A-B sets making three unit combinations possible where a 5400 HP set of two FT pairs were not needed. In Vermont, the Delaware & Hudson's new RS—2's appeared on their Rutland Branch, bringing dieseldom "under the nose" of all-steam Rutland. Also in 1946, the GE 70-ton switcher was first placed in operation by a New England road, the Belfast & Moosehead Lake.

The year 1947 marked the first significant diesel service on the Boston & Albany with the New York Central's purchase of Alco FA—1 and FB—1 sets for freight service. The N H also got the 1500 HP freighters in 1947 in fifteen A-B-A sets, augmenting the DL—109's already hauling freight. Other New Haven purchases were reorders of S—1's, 44-tonners, and the first New Haven RS—2's, which arrived with boilers for dual service. B & M and M E C got one 44-tonner each, the only unit bought by the B & M that year. The M E C got one S—1 and their first EMD F units; two A-B sets of boiler-equipped F—3's. The

NEW ENGLAND DIESELS

first Bangor & Aroostook diesels finally came in the form of two A-B-A sets of F-3's, a reversal of their previous committment to steam.

Steam continued to topple in 1948. The first New York Central PA's went into service handling passengers on the B & A, while more FA's were joining the freight pool. The New Haven also ordered the handsome PA-1, plus taking RS-1's and more RS-2's, each with boilers, and even more S-1 switchers. The B & M brought the EMD BL-2's into New England, acquiring four examples with boilers, but lacking MU controls, aimed at Boston commuter duties. The B & M also got their first F-3's, while reordering S-1's, E-7's and one 44-tonner. Still following B & M trends, Maine Central reordered E-7's and F-3's, while the B A R finished their buying of F-3's with two more A-B-A sets, two of the cab units with steam generators.

The Bangor & Aroostook increased the tempo of their dieselization in 1949 with the delivery of E-7's, NW-2's and eight BL-2's. Another steam stronghold fell in that year when the Canadian Pacific eliminated steam on its Vermont lines in a period of eight months with the arrival of four A-B-A sets of FA-1's, five RS-2's, three S-2's, and three E-8's, the latter to haul joint schedules with the B & M E-7's. This dieselization of C P's Lyndonville Subdivision was sort of a "test tube for diesels" on the C P and the successfulness of their experiment soon was evidenced in Ontario and across the system. The C P E-8's were unique to Canada and the first of that model in the area. The New Haven got the last of its 27 PA-1's in 1949, along with its final group of S-1's, bringing the total for that model to 65, the largest group of any one model in New England. The B & M received their only order for F-7's, four A-B sets, which became the only F-7's bought by a New England road. The B & M also got their first RS-2's, boiler equipped as were the BL-2's, plus E-7's, NW-2's, SW-1's, and S-1's, reorders in each case. Alco RS-2 demonstrator 1500 was sold to the B & M and retained that number. The M E C and P T shared an order for S-1's and S-2's and the M E C invested in its first road switchers; five RS-2's.

1950 saw eight diesel models introduced to New England rails as the pace of dieselization approached its apex. The New Haven bought the only Lima-Hamilton switchers owned by a New England road and these ten 1000 HP units were the N H's first purchase of large non-Alco engines. New Haven also brought the opposed-piston Fairbanks-Morse to their region one month later; ten Loewy-styled H-16-44 road switchers. The GP-7 became a resident as the B & M received eight of that then new model. The M E C got two S-4's and three SW-7's, both new types for New England. These SW-7's remained the only examples of that model in the area. The N Y C purchased sixteen 1000 HP Lima-Hamilton road switchers with boilers and assigned them to Boston commuter service. These were the only small road units that L-H ever built. N Y C also got early examples of Alco's S-3 and these found their way onto B & A lines. The D & H was buying RS-3's and they were running into Rutland, Vermont, but by this time the Rutland had been convinced and had started its dieselization with RS-3 200. Other roads getting RS-3's were the N H and N Y C. The B & M acquired its only E-8, four F-7 boosters to go with the A units of the previous year, and several S-3's and S-4's. The M E C and Bangor & Aroostook joined the B & M in buying GP-7's, and the Portland Terminal banished steam for good with the addition of S-4's. The P T acquired boiler equipped non-MU GP-7 1081 in 1950, and the unit was used in the B & M commuter pool in Boston. Perhaps this was for mileage equalization, since the B & M E units were used in pool service on M E C passenger schedules.

The diesel had its twentieth anniversity in New England in 1951. Few had dared to dream in 1931 that twenty years later, the steam locomotive would be in a "has been" category on most of the Northeast's railroads. Only two lines, the Grand Trunk and the Canadian Pacific lines in Maine had no diesel operations on their lines, while the Central Vermont had only their three S-2's. True, only the Portland Terminal was finished buying diesels but all the other roads were rapidly shutting the door on steam. Little Rutland moved quickly to dieselize its lines by re-ordering RS-3's, plus a group of smaller RS-1's and a single GE 70-tonner, the only 70-tonner owned by a major New England road. Rutland's neighbor, Central Vermont, bought its first diesel in nine years; a solitary S-4. Maine Central ordered the first SW-9 for the region in 1951, and it joined the SW-7's of 1950 in helper and local service on the Mountain Subdivision. All of the M E C's EMD switchers were equipped with MU at both ends for this service. M E C also reordered an S-4 and a GP-7. Alco's 1600 HP FA-2 and booster FB-2 arrived in New England on Alco-faithful New York Central in 1951. That same year the Boston & Albany was officially absorbed by the N Y C, with the 1939 vintage B & A HH-600's being re-numbered into the N Y C series. The N Y C also received its first E-8 units in that year. New Haven received RS-3's and a group of FB-2's from Alco (the N H never owned an FA-2) and began taking delivery of ten Fairbanks-Morse 2400 HP passenger C-liners with the B-A1A wheel arrangement. These were the New Haven's first non-Alco passenger units, after accumulating a fleet of eighty-seven DL-109's and PA-1's.

The Rutland Railway got four RS-3's in 1952, putting an end to steam operations. The Budd Rail Diesel Car made its appearance in New England in 1952 on the Boston & Maine. These first three RDC's were the beginning of what was to become the largest fleet of Budd cars. Absent from the diesel marketplace in 1951, the B & M made up for lost time in 1952, getting RS-3's and S-3's from Alco and GP-7's and SW-9's from EMD. The M E C and B A R each took small groups of GP-7's, while the New Haven finished up the task begun in 1931 with the remaining C-liners of its 1951 order and another group of RS-3's. The N H also sampled the RDC in 1952, becoming the second road in New England to own the self-propelled Budds. The New York Central got new batches of FA-2's, RS-3's, E-8's, and tried S-4's for the first time. The N Y C's power utilization in the region finally started to gel in the early 1950's. With diesels being so new, many large roads treated them like big steam power, with any particular class being found almost anywhere on the system. B & A passenger trains were pulled by Alco PA's, EMD E's, F-M Erie builts and even the rare Baldwin "babyface" passenger sets. Freights were forwarded with a variety of Alco, EMD, F-M, and Baldwin power, while Limas, and Alco hauled the commuters into Boston. The yards were primarily Alco, although Baldwin and F-M were to be seen. Within a few years, the Central saw the wisdom of assigning units of one builder to a specific area, and New England became home for FA's and RS-3's, E units for the varnish and Alco switchers in the yards.

The N Y C continued its past practices of buying RS-3's, E-8's, and S-4's in 1953, bringing the elimination of steam ever nearer. Boston & Maine bought only EMD products in the year 1953, taking GP-7's, SW-9's, New England's first SW-8's, and a large group of SW-1's. These switchers of 1953, even the 600 HP SW-1's were destined for local freight service rather than yard chores and arrived in road colors with large road-style number-boards. The B & M's mainline was dieselized and now the time had run out on the Moguls previously safe on the branches of New Hampshire! The RDC's continued to

NEW ENGLAND DIESELS

arrive during 1953..........The Maine Central got its only RS–3's and S–3's, two of each, plus more GP–7's and another SW–9 from EMD. Central Vermont added another S–4, still reluctant to invest in mainline diesels. Elsewhere, diesels were even being sold second-hand already! The N H's five Cooper-Bessemer engined switchers of 1936 and 1937 became the B A R's first non-EMD's. The New Haven's only delivery in 1953 was Budd RDC's, and this was the last original purchase before the replacement of diesels began. The New Haven roster now contained 70 Alco FA's and FB's, 97 Alco and F-M passenger units, 84 road switchers (RS–1's, RS–2's, RS–3's and H–16–44's) and 137 switchers.......Alcos, the 44-tonners, and the 10 Limas.

The Bangor & Aroostook had finished dieselization with the former New Haven switchers bought in 1953, but the potato traffic was just too much for the present diesel fleet to handle in the winter months. This led to the B A R leasing units during the potato rush and New Haven DL–109's and RS–2's hauled reefers at least one winter. The expense of leasing and the incompatibility of the Alco units, although not as costly as reactivating steam, convinced the B A R management to find a better solution. The answer came in 1954 in the form of the first GP–9's to call New England home. At least, part of the time, that is! The B A R purchased the five units after signing an agreement with the Pennsylvania Railroad that the B A R would use the units to move spuds in the winter, while the Pennsy used them for their summer rush moving the Great Lakes ore traffic. This arrangement worked out well, and in later years B A R GP–7's joined the GP–9's in Cleveland and elsewhere on the P R R. Other purchases in 1954 included M E C reordering S–4's. Apparently pleased with their GM switchers equipped for road local service, these Alcos came with MU on both ends and were ballasted for better tonnage ratings. Over the years, Maine Central has made much use of this equipment on the Alco and EMD switchers, with the EMD units even rated for the same tonnage as GP–7's on some of their railroad. The B & M got more RS–3's and their only Alco 251 model engines, a group of 800 HP S–5 switchers. Grand Trunk and Central Vermont received their first road diesels that year, each taking a pair of RS–3's. Although these were the first road units on the C V and first diesels on the G T, the parent C N's diesels had already started diesel road service on both lines. The first diesel movements on the Canadian Pacific's Maine lines took place in this period with Alco cab units and RS–3's.

Activity decreased in 1955 an the B & M received RS–3's 1518 and 1519; its last original diesels and last Alcos acquired new. Budd Company did well with the B & M in 1955, delivering 58 RDC's. The RDC's released road switchers from the North Station commuter runs and other passenger locals, enabling the road to finish the switch to diesels by reassigning existing units. The only other purchase in New England that year was two S–4's for C V.

However, the year 1956 would be one of great change on New England rails. Grand Trunk and Central Vermont ended steam operations with orders for GP–9's. The G T also received an S–4 and a pair of SW–900's, latter being the only SW–900's bought by a New England road. It is uncertain how much service these G T switchers actually saw on the Grand Trunk - New England lines. The C V got the G T's pair of RS–3's, probably in an attempt to keep like models together. The B & M bought still more RDC's, 34 units including 30 RDC–9's, a sort of "half-RDC–1" unique to the B & M. The RDC–9 had only one engine rather than the usual pair and no control stations. These were used to fill out multi-car consists with standard cars on the ends.

A major development of 1956 was the New Haven starting its second generation of diesel purchases; replacing diesels with diesels. Electro-Motive found favor this time with New Haven; GP–9's and SW–1200's arrived. These SW–1200's were equipped with Flexi-coil trucks and served on Shore Line locals initially and were the only units of this model bought by a region road. Alco contributed RS–11's (New England's first) and Fairbanks-Morse came in with H–16–44's in the new carbody. These acquisitions resulted in the retirement of about one-third of the DL–109's and several of the venerable Alco high-hoods. This did not add up to anywhere near eighty units, the number of new units purchased, and resulted in long lines of stored units, many of them less than ten years old. One is tempted to ask the reason for buying about fifty new units that were unneeded. The reason may lie in the corporate struggles that engulfed the N H management at this time. The same leadership woes led to the N H's purchase of the lightweight equipment. The first to arrive was the Pullman-Standard "Train X", powered by diesel-hydraulics of German design assembled by Baldwin. The other two lightweights arrived the next year, 1957.

Another N H transaction of 1956 brought the first two FL–9's on the property. These units, unique to the N H, ran as regular passenger diesels on the Boston to New York run until reaching the Park Avenue Tunnel in New York, when the prime mover would be shut down and the unit would continue by electric propulsion from the third rail. This enabled the N H to eliminate the engine swapping operation at New Haven from diesel to electric and vice-versa. The first two units came late in 1956 equipped with a Blomberg lead truck and an A-1-A Flexi-coil rear truck. Problems with clearances in third rail territory soon brought a two axle Flexi-coil to the front on the units, and all subsequent FL–9's have B–A-1-A Flexi-coils.

The only other buyer in 1956 was Maine Central for a pair of RS–11's, although possibly because of financial arrangements, one of the pair came as Portland Terminal 1082. The P T 1082 was used in M E C service with M E C 801, however.

The remaining lightweight trains ordered by the New Haven in 1956 were delivered in early 1957. The ACF Talgo Train was powered by Fairbanks-Morse, while the "Roger Williams" consisted of modified RDC's, with the end units having diesel-type streamlined cabs. The Boston & Maine also got into the act, receiving one Talgo trainset with F-M units, like the New Haven's. These were the only F-M's owned by the B & M. The B & M made more waves, though, by retiring its weary FT sets and replacing them with fifty GP–9's. The Geeps came in the new blue, black, and white scheme and were the first B & M road switchers bought without steam generators, aside from former demonstrator RS–2 1500. As "billboard" paint schemes were now spreading from boxcars to locomotive carbodies, these units brought this trend to New England, as did the black, orange, and white scheme of New Haven's new road switchers. The Grand Trunk finished buying diesels in 1957 with its last pair of GP–9's. The Maine Central received the two Portland Terminal road switchers in that year, the RS–11 becoming M E C 802 and the GP–7, M E C 581. Canadian Pacific began receiving MLW RS–18's, the Canadian version of the RS–11, and these started bumping the steamers off the line through Maine. The N H finished testing the FL–9 pair that came in 1956 and ordered 28 more, resulting in more DL–109's being stricken from the roster, and more units into storage.

In 1957, the Canadian Pacific acquired a large order of RS–18's and most steam operations ended in that year. Steam did manage to hold down a few runs into 1960, making Brownville Junction, Maine and CP's Mixed train,

NEW ENGLAND DIESELS

"The Scoot", the target of railfans. The years 1956 through 1958 offered interesting contrasts. While diesels replaced steam on the G T, C V, and C P, the same models were replacing older diesels on the N H and B & M. The only other transactions of 1958 were the B & M's final delivery of Budd cars and the Portland Terminal Company's takeover of the Greater Portland Public Development Commission trackage in South Portland, including an S-3, which became Portland Terminal 1101.

The late 1950's and early 1960's could be termed sad years as the passenger train followed the steam engine into oblivion at the hand of progress. Northern New England suffered hardest; first-class service ended on the B A R, M E C, G T, and only Budd cars remained on all but the Connecticut River line runs of the B & M. This made previously dual-use power available for freight service full time and the nearly thirty E-7's and E-8 of the B & M, M E C, and B A R surplus. The B A R innovated by re-gearing its two E-7's for freight service while the B & M sold its E-8 and stored its E-7's at its shops in Billerica, Massachusetts, before scrapping them. The Maine Central retained mail and express trains for a three-year period after passenger service ended in 1960, and this resulted in three E-7's retiring in 1960, one going to the Kansas City Southern and two cannibalized. Then, in the Fall of 1963, the remaining four were also sold to the K C S and were painted in bright K C S red and yellow by the M E C's Waterville Shops. They had been M E C's first group of E-7's, of 1946, and it might be said they left New England nearly as stylish as they had arrived!

The year 1959 was the first year since 1933 that no diesels were put into service in the region. The task of dieselization virtually complete, and the second generation diesels had not really come on the scene. Purchases in the next few years were sporadic. In 1960, the New Haven bought 30 more F L-9's, putting the remaining D L-109's out of service, along with the remaining C-liners and some P A-1's, as well as biting into the electric fleet. The Boston & Maine traded its unliked B L-2's in on G P-18's bringing the first low-nose units into New England. In 1963, the N Y C started running G P-35's into Boston and U-25-B's followed in 1964 — the trade-in momentum started on the Central. The Canadian National ordered six Grand Trunk Western SW-1200's to New England in 1963 and these road service equipped units worked wayfreights on both the C V and G T before settling on the C V. Most were re-painted in C V colors, by this year, that meant a version of C N's black, red, and white "new image". Three of these went back to the G T W in 1967 and 1968 but three still worked as Central Vermont 1509-1511. The New Haven placed its only order for "big" power in 1964 and received new U-25-B's and C-425's. What turned out to be N H's last order was New England's first and only Alco Century units, not considering those coming in on N Y C and Penn Central in later years as "natives".

In 1965, two roads received second-hand units. Maine Central got ex-Rock Island RS-3's 466 and 469 from General Electric, where they had been traded-in by the R I. The Central Vermont, which had had its RS-3's reassigned to parent C N for several years, had Alcos again in the shape of six Duluth Winnipeg & Pacific RS-11's. These also showed up on the Grand Trunk as maintenance of G T and C V power was now being performed at St. Albans, Vermont on the C V and both roads' engines were considered one pool. The RS-11's were repainted and stayed about three years before returning to the D W & P.

Early in 1966, the Bangor & Aroostook began its second generation of diesels by ordering a pair of the new EMD GP-38's. Neighbor Maine Central borrowed the pair

that summer, and, apparently impressed, started its second generation with a dozen GP-38's! This retired all M E C's F-3's and most of their RS-2's. Infant Vermont Railway getting "its feet placed" after taking over the Rutland, bought a new locomotive and a new model for the region, SW-1500, 501. Both B A R and M E C reordered the GP-38 in 1967, the M E C taking one, and the B A R trading its regeared E-7's, two NW-2's and two F-3's for six GP-38's.

The New York Central became half (?) of the Penn Central in 1968 and soon mixtures of N Y C and P R R units appeared. Units in Penn Central colors began to show up in New England as the P C took delivery of GP-40's and these became common to the old Boston & Albany line. The following year the New Haven went into the Penn Central and locomotive changes were major. The FL-9's soon departed their runs to Boston's South Station for New York City suburban service, being replaced by ex-P R R E-8's. Former Pennsy freight units streamed into New England, bringing models to the region never seen before. By 1972, most of these older RS-3's and switchers had been retired, with the balance of the old P R R power emmigrating elsewhere, being replaced by new GP-38's, SW-1500's, and GP-38-2's.

The Vermont Railway received its first GP-38-2 in 1972, and in that year, the Bangor & Aroostook went shopping on the used-locomotive market. In the Fall of 1972, the B A R bought ten SW-9's from the Pittsburgh & Lake Erie and Pittsburgh, Youghiogheny & Chartiers to supplement its leasing fleet. Later in the year, in an attempt to acquire a steel snowplow from a Canadian industry, the B A R got more than it anticipated; in additional to the plow, it got a GE 65-ton centercab and a former Canadian built S-3. Since then, both of the small units and most of the SW-9's have been resold to the US and Canada.

The Boston & Maine received its first new power in a dozen years with the purchase of a dozen GP-38-2's in 1973. New England captured another first in 1974 as the Providence & Worcester, itself one year old as an independent railroad, took delivery of the first Canadian built diesels to be imported new to the United States. The two M-420W's replaced leased D & H RS-3's which the P & W had begun operations with. A reorder in 1975 for three more M-420W's sent the balance of the RS-3's home. This made the P & W's roster all MLW.

Canadian National M-420W's appeared on the Grand Trunk in 1975, replacing C N GP-9's and RS-18's then being used on the Montreal - Portland through freight. This change eliminated power changes and layovers at the terminal in Richmond, Quebec, with the same units now running through from Montreal to Portland. July, 1975, brought another new model to the region as the Maine Central invested in ten U-18-B's from GE. The first U-18's in the Northeast, the M E C's "baby boats" carry the color scheme initiated with the GP-38's of 1966 and have replaced Alco yard and road switchers of the 1940's.

This Bicentennial year marks the 45th anniversary of the diesel in New England. Except for the Penn Central old N H electrification, the conquest of internal combustion has been complete. In 1976, the original units that bumped steam are getting harder to find, except for the ubiquitous Geep. As we look forward, it looks certain that those old New England Yankee traits of independence (M E C's recent break from EMD), strong ties with the past (B A R's remarkable F-3's and BL-2's, C P's original RS-2's), Yankee ingenuity (P & W's imported "better idea"), and good old Downeast stubborness (B & M's 35 year old pre-war NW-2's refusal to quit) will continue to be exhibited by the railroads of this great region.

NEW ENGLAND DIESELS

MAINE

Ronald N. Johnson

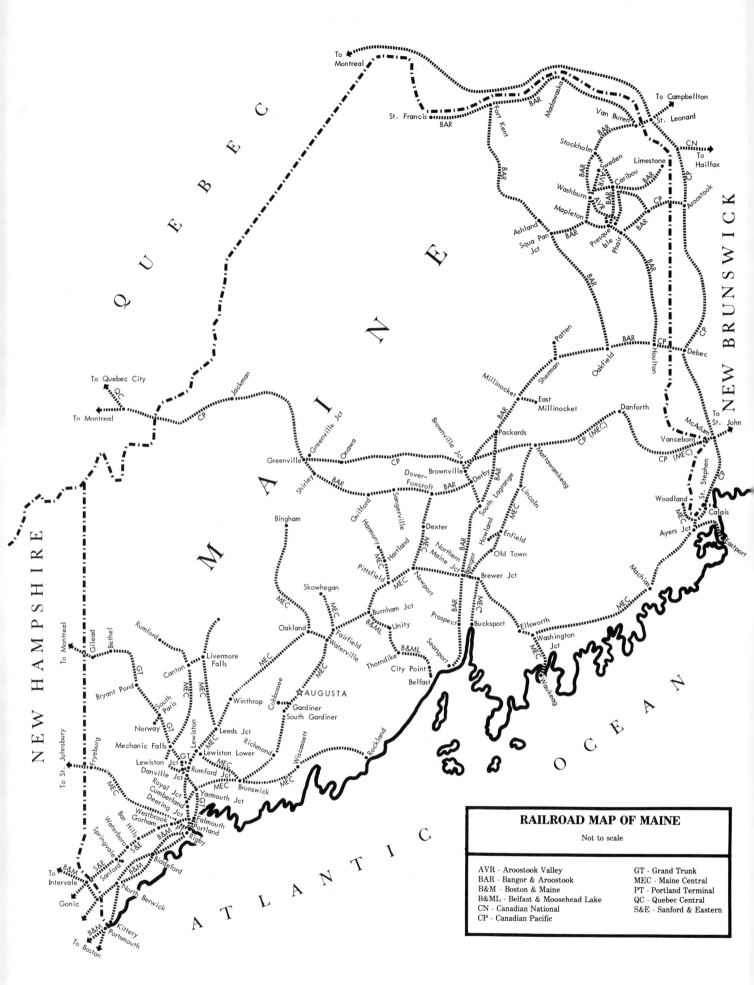

RAILROAD MAP OF MAINE

Not to scale

AVR - Aroostook Valley	GT - Grand Trunk
BAR - Bangor & Aroostook	MEC - Maine Central
B&M - Boston & Maine	PT - Portland Terminal
B&ML - Belfast & Moosehead Lake	QC - Quebec Central
CN - Canadian National	S&E - Sanford & Eastern
CP - Canadian Pacific	

NEW ENGLAND DIESELS

12

Bangor & Aroostook GP-7 works empty pulpwood racks east on the St. Francis Branch near St. John, Maine in October 1975. In the background is the St. John River and rural Connors, New Brunswick. *(Robert C. Baker, Jr.)*

Resting near the old enginehouse at Fort Kent, SW-9 #34 is assigned to the branch this day. *(Dave Albert)*

S-3 #20, the only Alco ever owned by the Bangor & Aroostook, idles between local and mill switching assignments beside the Fraser Paper Company at Madawaska, Maine. Built by the Montreal Locomotive Works as Canadian National 8485 and later as Fraser Paper #7, 20 is now in Ohio with its fourth owner. *(George Melvin)*

In this and the two facing photos, George Melvin records an interesting three-way meet at Ashland, Maine on April 7, 1973. BL-2 55 arrives with south-bound freight No. 212 out of Madawaska for Oakfield. The local, which has preceeded No. 212, waits in the hole.

After setting off, the pair of blue and yellow units chant past the old station and back onto the main. Still plenty of snow in April!

No. 212 has now picked up the local with #63 in the lead and also BL-2 #57 from No. 211 North which now passes on the mainline bound for Madawaska.

GP-7 #75 backs its train of pulpwood into the yard at Caribou after finishing a run on local No. 84 to Mapleton and the Wasburn Cut-off on July 12, 1971. *(Paul Westin)*

Freight No. 58 swings off the east leg of the wye at Squa Pan Junction. Lead unit #42 wears the new "tri-color" paint scheme of dark blue, orange, and grey with yellow striping and silver trucks. No. 58 out of Caribou traverses the mainline to Presque Isle, then over the Mapleton Cut-off and Mapleton Branch to Squa Pan, and down the Ashland Branch to Oakfield. *(Dave Albert)*

A Canadian Pacific wayfreight works west at Fort Fairfield, Maine in the winter of 1974. The branch from Aroostook Junction in New Brunswick and a thirteen mile Bangor & Aroostook branch serves the town. *(George Pitarys)*

Tile roofed stations and potato houses are common sights along the Bangor & Aroostook as we see here in Presque Isle as the wayfreight arrives in town. Wearing the original colors, #56 is trailed by one of the ex-troop sleeper bay-window cabooses. *(Walker Transportation Collection—Beverly Historical Society)*

Two-thirds of Aroostook Valley Railroad's blue and yellow MU-equipped 44 tonners roll the daily freight into Washburn, Maine enroute from Presque Isle to Caribou on October 9, 1969. Although the Aroostook Valley is owned by the Canadian Pacific, interchange business with the Bangor & Aroostook is substantial as we see below when GP-7 62 with the local out of Presque Isle hauls into Washburn to meet the AVR. *(Both photos by Herman Shaner)*

Northbound Doodlebug. Diesel Railcar #5 accelerates the local out of Oakfield, bound for Fort Kent over the scenic Ashland branch. It will skirt 95 miles of the vast Allagash wilderness; playground for sportsmen and a source of timber for Maine's major industry. Formerly Great Northern #2341 built by Westinghouse in 1930, #5 served this run from February to August 31, 1954 when this train was discontinued. *(Russ Munroe, Jr.)*

The summer evening shadows grow longer as "The Potatoland" makes its station stop at Oakfield in this July 1950 scene with new E-7 #701 in charge. Along with sister #700, she handled this train and northbound companion "Aroostook Flyer." With the addition of stainless steel streamlined equipment, travelers experienced the finest first class accommodations, dining and sleeping facilities of any road in the northeast. *(Photo courtesy of Bangor & Aroostook R.R.)*

NW-2 #23 is ready for night duty at Oakfield, Maine, an important yard and division point on the Bangor & Aroostook. *(Beverly Historical Society)*

With GP-38 #81 on the point, freight No. 44 gets rolling upgrade out of the yard on April 12, 1972. The solid train of pulpwood is bound for Northern Maine Junction and Maine Central points to the south. *(George Melvin)*

Switching the yard at Oakfield can be more than a single yard engine can handle, so #87 and #66 have teamed up to move the heavy cuts of cars. (Dave Albert)

In the waning days of steam power, a southbound freight blasts out of Millinocket with the 505 getting an assist from a 400 series 4-8-2. (Russ Munroe, Jr. Beverly Historical Society)

Bathed in steam at Millinocket in 1951 is the Second section of the "Potatoland Special." Shortly, the 507 will ease out of the snow-plugged yard for Van Buren and a battle with the drifts of a rugged Aroostook County winter. *(Russ Munroe, Jr.—Beverly Historical Society Collection)*

While a group of passengers await their train, the operator stands ready with orders for the southbound "Aroostook Flyer." Over on the adjoining track is the East Millinocket local with its ancient combine-coach. *(Photo Courtesy of Bangor & Aroostook R.R.)*

No. 51 eases a string of cars into the giant mills of the Great Northern Paper Co. at East Millinocket. The date, June 20, 1963, and the mixed train has long since vanished. A caboose (second car from engine), a former troop sleeper has replaced the venerable combine.

At the end of the day's chores, the 51 is turned on the "armstrong" turntable for the run back to Millinocket. *(Frank DiFalco)*

F-3 #503 handles the southbound local at Packards, the junction of the old Brownville mainline and the Medford Cutoff. *(Photo courtesy of Bangor & Aroostook)*

The Greenville Branch local clatters into the yard at Derby, Maine. Although it is September 7, 1955, one can sense the antiquity of the scene; a rare engine, an old wooden boxcar and baggage car for caboose, framed in the eaves of an old station and order board.

E-7 #10 and a pair of F-3's lead a southbound freight past the manicured lawns of the road's car shops at Derby. After the demise of passenger service, the 10 and 11 got a new lease on life and were re-geared for freight service. Both disappeared from the roster in 1967 as trade-ins for GP-38's. *(Both photos by Jim Shaughnessy)*

No. 981 wheels into Jackman, Maine behind RS-18 #8735, an RS-3 and two FB units on August 1, 1965. *(George Melvin)*

An eastbound freight in charge of #8456, rumbles over the awesome trestle at Onawa, Maine. *(Russ Munroe, Jr.)*

The Bangor & Aroostook local with a cut of interchange cars arrives at the Canadian Pacific yard at Brownville Junction. Steam still prevails here as a Mike tussles with a string of cars in the distance. *(Jim Shaughnessy)*

In the pre-dawn, sub-zero darkness, Canadian Pacific's eastbound Train 42, the "Atlantic Limited" stands at the Brownville Junction station in March of 1975. The Northeast's version of the "California Zephyr" complete with dome car, has just passed its westbound companion in the remote wilderness east of Greenville. *(Frank DiFalco)*

Westbound mixed train #517, "The Scoot" with its trailing combine and caboose awaits a "highball" at the station at Brownville Junction on December 30, 1966. Over on the right, S-2 #7097 works the yard. This train was a favorite for hunters and fishermen. *(George Melvin)*

To the southwest of the Canadian Pacific's Onawa trestle stands another structure of equal proportions. The Bangor & Aroostook trestle over Bunker Brook near Shirley, Maine on the Greenville branch carries a slow board, so BL-2 #56 eases across with the local. The mixed train ran for a while after the arrival of the diesels, but was later discontinued. Dwindling freight revenues and extensive cost of bridge repairs brought about piecemeal abandonment between 1959 and 1965. *(Wayne E. Duplisea)*

Maine Central freight VB-2 rounds the curve into Mattawamkeag with RS-3's 557 and 556 on the point. Out of Vanceboro at dawn, the Bangor bound train will meet its eastbound counterpart, BV-1, somewhere down the line. The Maine Central and Canadian Pacific still share the 58 miles of iron between Mattawamkeag and Vanceboro in this 1969 scene. *(Dave Albert)*

Canadian Pacific's No. 1800 heads Train 42, "The Atlantic Limited" in the early morning hours at Danforth on the Maine Central. Sporting the new candy-stripe CP Rail colors, the E-8 and her seven-car consist has one more stop at Vanceboro before crossing the border. *(George Pitarys)*

With the first rays of the morning sun striking off the cab, Maine Central 44 tonner 13 has finished its night-shift switching at Vanceboro yard and is headed for the roundhouse on April 29, 1972. She has since finished her days on the Maine Central and the 58 miles of joint trackage including Vanceboro yard is now owned by the Candadian Pacific. *(George Melvin)*

Dawn of a bright spring day finds Canadian Pacific's Train 42, the eastbound "Atlantic Limited" gliding into Vanceboro after an overnight journey across Maine. E-8 1802 leads the five-car consist which includes a dome-car and RDC 9069 bringing up the rear enroute for an engine swap on the Dominion & Atlantic. *(Dave Albert)*

Extra 8749 East brakes to a stop at the Maine Central station at Vanceboro after its run over the joint trackage in March of 1966. With two RS-18's powering sixty loads of export wheat for St. John, New Brunswick, this is called a "Grainbox" by the Canadian Pacific. At sunset, below, Maine Central's local freight, BV-1, from Bangor, slides into the Vanceboro yard with RS-2's 555 and 551. *(Both photos George Melvin)*

In its last year of operation, photographer Jim Shaughnessy lensed the Derby-Guilford local, a remnant of the old Greenville branch. Above, NW-2 #22 rattles past the old highway covered bridge at Sangerville on the westward leg of the run on August 28, 1964. On the return trip, below, she has two cars in tow.

The bright snow reflects off the gleaming flanks of the recently delivered 503 as it handles a southbound potato extra off the Medford Cutoff at South Lagrange in 1948. The Brownville mainline is to the left. *(Photo courtesy Bangor & Aroostook)*

A trio of F-3's lead northbound symbol freight NO-55 at South Lagrange in 1964. *(Frank DiFalco)*

Maine Central's first diesel road unit, #901, a 600 HP R.P.O.— Baggage Car shown here at Bangor in 1940. Built by Ingersoll-Rand in 1933 as Demonstrator OE-600, the 110 ton railcar was placed in passenger service on the Vanceboro line in 1935; usually with a coach or two. Bumped by the E-7's in 1947, the 901 handled the local between Lewiston and Rumford until retirement in 1949. The ghost of the 901 still haunts the rails today as Tool Car 950. *(Collection of Russ Munroe, Jr.)*

GP-7 #571 works the Lincoln Extra east on the Vanceboro branch along the Penobscot River above Bangor in 1969. *(Dave Albert)*

Westbound freight CB-2 pauses for orders at Machias on the Calais branch on October 24, 1952. The arrival of five Alco RS-2's in 1949, followed by a pair of RS-3's in 1953 completed dieselization on the Eastern Division.

Maine Central's engine terminal at Bangor services a wide variety of road power, for this is the principal locomotive inspection and light repair facility. This group has been gathered for an "official portrait" around the table. *(Both photos courtesy of Maine Central)*

The easternmost railroad milepost in the United States at Eastport, Maine. This 16 mile branch has one of the few remaining GE 44 Ton switchers in regular freight service on a Class I road. Light rail prompted the use of this type since the coming of the diesel. Here #16 is busy at the Key Street yard about a mile from the docks and fish canneries in June of 1954. *(J. Emmons Lancaster)*

Train No. 116 is ready to depart Calais on the 133 mile run to Bangor in the last month of passenger service on the branch in May of 1956. *(Photo courtesy Maine Central)*

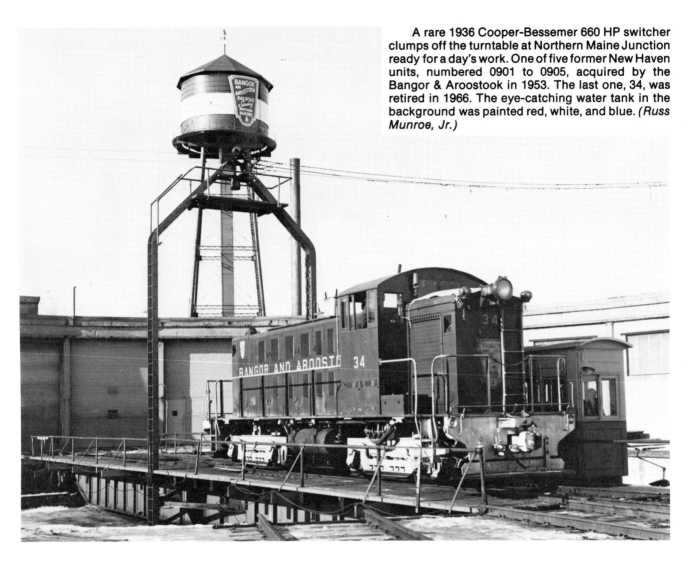

A rare 1936 Cooper-Bessemer 660 HP switcher clumps off the turntable at Northern Maine Junction ready for a day's work. One of five former New Haven units, numbered 0901 to 0905, acquired by the Bangor & Aroostook in 1953. The last one, 34, was retired in 1966. The eye-catching water tank in the background was painted red, white, and blue. *(Russ Munroe, Jr.)*

Looking like a retirement home for old diesels, a group of F-3's and BL-2's are gathered on the service tracks at the Junction in the summer of 1969. The engine terminal is also the locomotive repair shop. *(Dave Albert)*

Train No. 2 is about to enter the Maine Central mainline at Northern Maine Junction to finish the last five miles of its run to Bangor Union Station. It is August of 1960 and the Bangor & Aroostook is near to being "freight only." *(Herman Shaner)*

A westbound freight slips across the spindly trestle at Prospect, Maine on the Searsport branch on December 27, 1975. *(Ronald N. Johnson)*

Maine Central's SW-7's 331 and 333 move upgrade out of Bucksport with tonnage for Bangor in December of 1974. The branch sees two trains daily and it is not uncommon to find all five of the road's SW series on the line on the same day. *(Ronald N. Johnson)*

Penobscot Bay and the piers form a backdrop for the 56 and 83 as they make up their train at Searsport. Over the years, this rail-sea terminal has handled coal, grain, salt, chemicals, oil products, paper, and agricultural products providing a healthy flow of traffic to the Bangor & Aroostook. *(Jim Shaughnessy)*

A pair of Alco S-2's cast a reflection on an inlet of Lake Wassookeag at Dexter, Maine as they work the tri-weekly local west on the Dover-Foxcroft branch. *(George Melvin)*

Remnant of a once proud train! After the demise of passenger service in 1960, the Maine Central introduced fast "merchandise-mail" trains. Train #8, the former "Gull," gets underway after picking up milk cars at Newport Junction on September 5, 1961. The service was discontinued in 1963 and some of the E-7's went west to the Kansas City Southern. *(Kenneth S. MacDonald)*

Opposing schedules of the "Kennebec Limited" meet in a summer thundershower at Pittsfield, Maine in 1950. Boston & Maine #3806 on Train No. 12 is working off mileage on the Maine Central under the joint power pool agreement. The scene was shot from the express car door of No. 11 by then Railway Express man Herm Shaner.

A friendly game of horseshoes by the Belfast crew is underway at the Junction. The 51 idles on the team track while waiting for the Maine Central connection. This quiet scene on June 13, 1954 will later be interrupted by a blast of a steam whistle and the passing of Pacific #470 on the last steam run. *(Collection of 470 Railroad Club)*

No. 52 accelerates across the Sebasticook River bridge out of Burnham Junction eastbound for Belfast.

By the mid-1950's, the regular passenger train gave way to mixed train service lasting until 1961. Here, #52 clatters over a highway crossing on its way back to Belfast. *(Both photos Russ Munroe, Jr., Walker Transportation Collection—Beverly Historical Society)*

Sea gulls and salt air marks the home terminal at Belfast. No. 51 is busy with yard chores and making up the wayfreight. In the background is the tugboat "Seguin," one of the last steam tugs in operation on the East coast. *(Walker Transportation Collection—Beverly Historical Society)*

Handling the freight on the 33 "hill and dale" miles sometimes calls for two or three of the 70 Tonners. No. 52, along with 50 on the rear, rumbles onto the bridge at City Point, a few miles above Belfast. *(Ronald N. Johnson)*

The autumn air is crisp as local freight WP-1 rumbles across the bridge over the Kennebec River between Fairfield and Benton in September of 1968. The huge structure stands 50 feet above the water and stretches nearly 2000 feet from shore to shore. The hard working S-4 is accelerating for the run to Newport and Hartland. *(Dave Albert)*

Hotshot! Westbound B-12 Extra kicks up dust as it races through Waterville. The original batch of 20 GP-7's still remain on the roster today, although the maroon and yellow colors of Boston & Maine influence have given way to green and now "new image" yellow. *(Horace W. Pontin)*

Old S-1 #956 is busy making up the eastbounds at Waterville Yard in 1971. A dozen of these 660 HP diesel switchers replaced aging 0-6-0's along the system in the 1940's. Today only four remain on the roster. *(Dave Albert)*

In 1956, the need for two additional locomotives sent the Maine Central shopping and lo and behold, they came home with a pair of "notched nosed" Alco RS-11's. Frequently seen on the mainline jobs nowadays the pair spent most of their life on the branches hauling the wood trains. Here at Oakland, Maine, they have just brought HW-2 down off the Bingham branch and have "changed ends" for the run back to Waterville *(Inset)* where they layover between runs. *(Dave Albert — Inset George Melvin)*

Camp Train! GP-7 573 wheels through Winthrop on August 18, 1966 with five empty New Haven coaches for North Anson on the Bingham branch. A group of handicapped youngsters, who have spent the summer at camp, will be making the trip home. *(Frank DiFalco photo—Jay Potter collection)*

Representing the first new power purchased in a decade, the Maine Central in 1966-1967 took delivery of thirteen bright yellow GP-38's; thus embarking on a "new image" program. B-11 East pounds through Leeds Junction with the 251 and 252 on the point while the 261 and 262 holds the siding with DR-2 off the Rumford branch. *(Dave Albert)*

The daily Rumford-Portland freight, DR-2, with F3's 685 and 671, picks up outgoing loads of paper from International Paper's Otis Mill at Livermore Falls. Eight train movements a day makes this branch the busiest on the Maine Central. *(George Melvin)*

The Farmington local is light today as the 576 whips through Wilton on October 14, 1969. This 16 mile branch leaves the Rumford line at Livermore Falls. *(Dave Albert)*

46

Symbol freight B-12 winds along the Kennebec River valley near South Gardiner on the "Lower Road" mainline. The road's first freight diesels, 672 A&B and 671 A&B, have teamed up to move the 100 car manifest bound for Rigby Yard. *(George Melvin)*

With the crew perched precariously atop the boxcar, #15 eases over the trestle after a trip up the Cobbossee branch at Gardiner. Below, the raging waters of Cobbossee Stream boil around the pilings. *(Photo courtesy Maine Central)*

Boston & Maine 1140 arrives at Brunswick, Maine with "The Mate" in 1937. With a few exceptions, this Ingersoll-Rand unit was nearly identical to Maine Central's 901. The 1930's saw the beginning of the joint power pool between the two roads and although Boston & Maine steam power became a common sight all the way to Bangor, the visit of the 1140 on the Rockland bound train was a rare occurrence. *(Howard Kirkpatrick)*

A polished 44 tonner muscles a cut of cars in the west yard. Brunswick, on the "Lower Road" mainline, is the junction point for the 20 mile Lewiston Branch and the 57 mile line to Rockland. These rugged midgets such as the 14, were ideal at the small terminals. *(Photo courtesy Maine Central)*

Eastbound Extra 561 for Augusta holds the main while RA-1 for Lewiston with the 563 moves up alongside in the west yard on May 23, 1970. *(Dave Albert)*

What's this! Photographer Robert Baker, Sr. stepped out of his home at Harding's near Brunswick to snap a shiny new RS-3 on eastbound Train 57 for Rockland. The recently-delivered 557 was breaking in on the branch before being transferred to the Eastern Division. After 22 years of service, she was sold in 1976 to the Wolfboro R.R. for use on their Lincoln Branch in New Hampshire.

During their brief assignment to the Grand Trunk, RS-3's 1861 and 1862 usually worked the Portland to Gorham, N.H. wayfreights. Here, they meet at Bryant Pond, Maine on October 29, 1955. *(470 Railroad Club)*

Following on the heels of the Providence & Worcester, new M420's have ventured across the border onto the Grand Trunk. Train 393 barrels through the fresh snow at Gilead, Maine on March 9, 1975. *(Ronald N. Johnson)*

Train 214, the Rumford-Portland local, nears Danville Junction on a sunny July morning in 1953. The versatile "geeps" were right at home on the branch line trains. *(Edward P. Street, Jr.)*

Grand Trunk RS-3 1862 switches out a cut of cars over the Maine Central diamond at Danville Junction while working No. 749, the Portland-Gorham local, in 1955. *(Herman Shaner)*

Canadian National's FPA-4's never looked classier than in this view of a pair leaving Yarmouth Junction with the Montreal-bound "summer-only" passenger extra of July 4, 1962. *(Herman Shaner)*

Running hours late due to snow, No. 394 roars past the old station at Yarmouth in March of 1971. *(George Melvin)*

Eastbound Train 15, "Flying Yankee," sweeps around the curve near Royal Junction in the summer of 1956. The introduction of streamlined stainless steel equipment in 1947 added a touch of class to Maine Central's passenger fleet.

The chant of 6000 horsepower fills the air as westbound freight B-12 moves through Yarmouth, Maine with 156 cars on July 19, 1956. *(Both photos courtesy Maine Central)*

New E-7 706 heads No. 14 "Pine Tree" west along the double track at Cumberland, Maine in 1946. The 706 wears the short-lived "Rock Island" style colors, an experiment to make the first four E-7's delivered compatible with the new stainless steel coaches. By 1948, all were repainted in the Boston & Maine style maroon and yellow.

Train No. 11, the "Kennebec" approaches the North Deering section of Portland; its journey from Bangor nearly over. The decline of patrons can be seen in comparison with the eleven cars of the above "Pine Tree." *(Both photos courtesy Maine Central)*

RS-3 #1826 and the Instruction Car reposes near the enginehouse at East Deering on September 25, 1954. The unit is here for five days of "crew familiarization" with the new diesels soon to arrive. The 1826 arrived from Montreal in operation with Mikado #3715, and it is believed to have been the first steam-diesel double-header of which many were to follow. *(John Egan collection)*

Filled with Canadian tourists headed for Maine's beaches, the "summer only" passenger extra rolls through Falmouth with RS-18's #3111 and 3118 in August of 1965. This train was introduced in the summer months to handle the tourist traffic after the discontinuance of the daily train in 1960. The summer trains eventually made their last runs in 1966. *(George Melvin)*

A slow board is the rule as the Grand Trunk's Portland-Lewiston wayfreight creaks over the trestle-swing bridge spanning Portland's Back Cove on February 17, 1975. *(Ronald N. Johnson)*

Grand Trunk #4902 stands ready to depart the India Street station in Portland with No. 17 for Montreal in August of 1960. The train still rates five cars in this scene, but the end is near as the final runs of No. 16 and 17 took place on September 5th. *(Dwight A. Smith)*

The "State of Maine Express" passes Tower 3 at River Junction on the approach to Portland Union Station on April 17, 1950. Located in the middle of Fore River, the tower controlled the cross-overs and diamond on the two sets of tracks for the Boston mainline and the Mountain Sub-division to the right. Several years later, a new bridge and track relocation erased this scene.

The Boston section of the "Kennebec" eases out of the trainshed at Portland on July 20, 1957. Maine Central's general office building looms in the background. *(Both photos Wayne D. Allen collection)*

Veteran switcher 1003, Alco Class of 1936, makes up an afternoon train in the west coach yard in the summer of 1952. The old ball signal to the left was later donated to the Baltimore & Ohio Museum at Baltimore. *(470 Railroad Club)*

Pioneer diesel streamliner 6000 arrives in Portland for public display while on tour in April of 1934. A near duplicate of Burlington's "Zephyr," introduced a few months earlier, the 6000 ushered in a new era of railroading in the Northeast. She was placed in service on the Boston to Bangor run as the "Flying Yankee" from 1934 to 1945, then replaced by a conventional train. *(Walker Transportation Collection—Beverly Historical Society)*

The Alco 600 HP High-hood switcher found favor on the Portland Terminal with the acquisition of four such units, numbered 1001 to 1004, in 1936. They were ideal for switching the warehouses and piers along the waterfront district because of their short wheelbase. Here, the 1001, trundles a coal train down Commercial Street on April 14, 1939. *(Howard Kirkpatrick)*

Maine Central's first diesel switchers were a pair of Alco 660 HP High-hoods, numbered 951-952, acquired in 1938. They were frequently seen over the years working the Bangor, Waterville, and Brunswick yards. The 952 spent her final years on lease to the Portland Terminal, and is seen here leaving Yard No. 8 on West Commercial Street with a transfer run for Rigby Yard in 1965. *(George Melvin)*

Portland Terminal's wayward GP-7 #1081 takes a break at the Boston & Maine enginehouse at Charlestown, Mass. in 1955. On lease to the Boston & Maine, the 1081 was used principally as a "mileage equalizer" for the Maine Central and was frequently seen on commuter runs in the Boston and Portsmouth area. In 1956, she was transferred to the Maine Central and renumbered to 581. *(Dave Albert collection)*

New RS-11 #1082, shown here at Rigby Yard, South Portland on July 10, 1956, was probably an arrangement between the two roads. Within a few months, the unit was renumbered 802 and transferred to the Maine Central to join sister 801. *(Photo courtesy Maine Central)*

Operator's view toward Boston from Tower One at Rigby Yard in 1946 found nearly-new diesel power in charge; E-7 3806 rolls up the eastbound main with Portland local #123 while symbol freight M-6 with an FT A-B-B-A set, waits for a highball to start its run to Worcester. *(Herman Shaner)*

Portland Terminal workhorse #1006 glides through the switches near Tower Two at the east end of Rigby in 1952. Seventeen Alco switchers operating over 128 miles of terminal trackage serve parent Maine Central and the Boston & Maine. *(Dave Albert collection)*

The 113 bustles about the Biddeford yard on a bright August day in 1951. A local switcher was assigned here for many years and often as not, it was a 44 tonner. *(470 Railroad Club)*

GP-9 1726 leading an old B-unit and a sister engine, highballs along the Portland Division mainline near Biddeford in 1964. The double track has now reverted to single iron. *(Russ Munroe, Jr.)*

Born in 1949, the Sanford & Eastern Railroad, a Sam Pinsly line, operated over a revived segment of the Boston & Maine's old Worcester, Nashua, and Portland line. Above, at Cumberland Mills near Westbrook, the 14 and a caboose of undoubtedly B&M ancestry, wait at the diamond crossing over the Maine Central Mountain Subdivision. *(Norton D. Clark)*

The local, with the 14 in charge, crosses the Saco River at Bar Mills in 1960. *(Russ Munroe, Jr.)*

The Waterboro station, long boarded-up and shorn of its order boards, sits silently as the freight arrives in town in 1959. The 9 was formerly of the Saratoga & Schuylerville, a New York shortline.

The 9 switches the yard at Springvale in the last months of operation in 1960. After abandonment, the 70 tonner hightailed it for the Claremont & Concord in New Hampshire. *(Both photos Russ Munroe, Jr.)*

NEW HAMPSHIRE

Dwight A. Smith

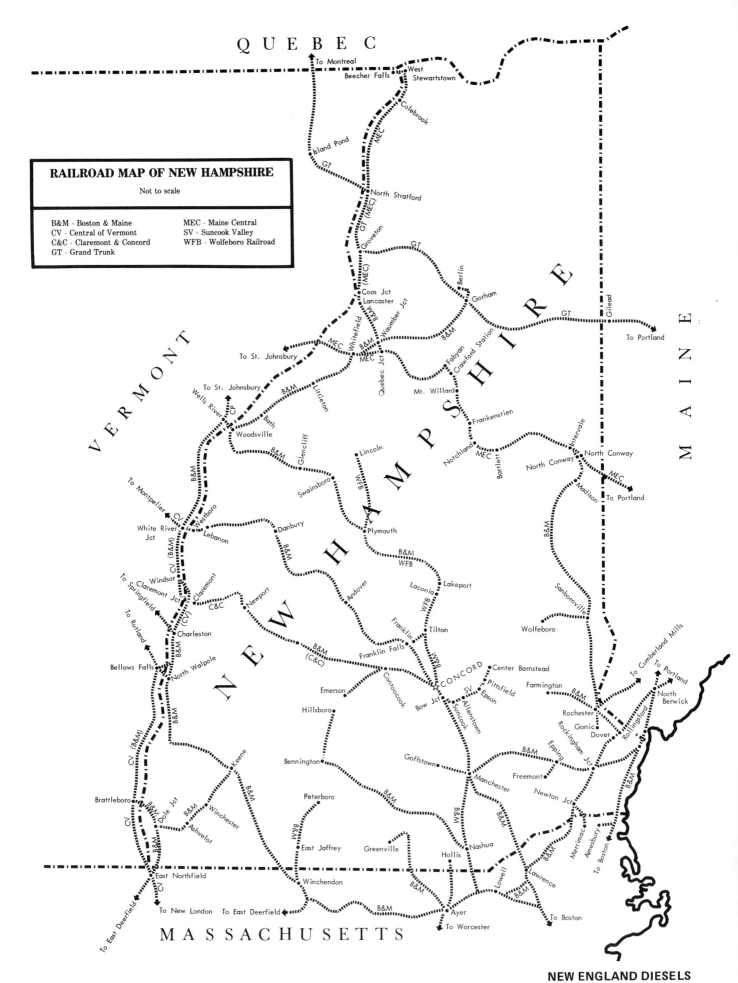

RAILROAD MAP OF NEW HAMPSHIRE

Not to scale

B&M - Boston & Maine
CV - Central of Vermont
C&C - Claremont & Concord
GT - Grand Trunk

MEC - Maine Central
SV - Suncook Valley
WFB - Wolfeboro Railroad

QUEBEC

VERMONT

NEW HAMPSHIRE

MAINE

MASSACHUSETTS

NEW ENGLAND DIESELS

In later years, the GP-7's took over the chores on the 58 mile branch. With only four cars out of Beecher Falls this day, the 568 glides through the snow-covered fields near Colebrook in February of 1975. *(Dave Albert)*

Jim Shaughnessy captured this breath-taking view of Maine Central's mixed train No. 377 on the Beecher Falls branch in May of 1954. The train is about to cross the Connecticut River into West Stewartstown for the remainder of the run in New Hampshire. The 334 is one of five GM-EMD 1200 HP units that bumped the Class "O" tenwheelers off the branch in 1951.

Arriving at North Stratford, Train 377 will operate on trackage rights over the Grand Trunk to Groveton where it will "change ends" and run over the Boston & Maine line to Coos Junction near Lancaster. The remainder of the trip will be over its own iron to Quebec Junction. The brakeman relaxes in the combine during the stop here for orders. Since the removal of Maine Central's own station, the road maintains an "open air" order board with the crews booking in at the Grand Trunk station across the yard. The mixed trains were discontinued in 1955. (Both photos Jim Shaughnessy)

The Grand Trunk local from Island Pond, Vermont takes the siding at Berlin, N.H. for an eastbound passenger extra on July 7, 1973. Switching the Brown Company paper mill here, will be the first order of business before returning to Island Pond. *(Dave Albert)*

With 110 January miles now behind the markers, JU-1 drags into Berlin with GP18 1750 and F7A 4265. JU-1 is the daily freight from White River Junction to Berlin; Boston & Maine's northernmost line. *(George Melvin)*

Boston & Maine GP-7 #1557 wyes the cars of train #4301 in the Berlin yard on April 8, 1952. This train will go out later as #4308. F-7 units #4265 A&B and #4268B wait by the enginehouse to follow #4308 south with freight DJ-2. *(Philip R. Hastings)*

Across the river at Cascade, Grand Trunk freight 393 climbs upgrade towards Berlin. A pair of M420's spliced with a GP-9 provides plenty of power to get the train through the rugged mountains that form the Androscoggin River valley in northern New Hampshire. *(Ronald N. Johnson)*

Westbound freight UJ-2 for White River Junction roars out of Berlin over the long trestle spanning the Androscoggin River and Route 16 at Gorham in 1964. *(Russ Munroe, Jr.)*

Train 16 for Portland, Maine makes its stop at Gorham in July of 1960. In the background, the silent enginehouse, shops, and coal pocket remind one of Gorham's one-time importance as a division point. *(Walker Transportation Collection—Beverly Historical Society)*

A coal strike brought diesels to Maine Central's Mountain Subdivision for the first time in February of 1950. Here, at Bartlett, F-3 #682 and #683 have come back down the mountain with 2-8-2 #626 after taking the first section of freight #375 up to Crawford Notch. Tenwheeler #369 is being serviced by the enginehouse and #371 is making up Train M378 for Beecher Falls on the right. *(Philip R. Hastings)*

By the end of 1950, the delivery of three SW-7's and some boiler-equipped GP-7's for passenger service displaced all steam power on the division. Here, the Gilman Extra is preparing to leave the lower yard at Bartlett with the 331 and 334 in 1952. These units carried extra weight for helper service up through the Notch. *(Photo courtesy Maine Central)*

Perched high on the rugged cliffs of Crawford Notch is the Mount Willard Dwelling, a former home for Maine Central track crews. The house maintains its lonely vigil as Train 162 for St. Johnsbury, Vermont passes on its way to the summit. Ahead, the rocky shoulder of Mount Webster attests to the fact that this is one of the most scenic railroad lines in the Northeast. *(Jim Shaughnessy)*

Mountain Battlers! Westbound RY-2, above, is down to a crawl on the Willey Brook bridge as they fight the 2.75% grade near Mount Willard in 1967. In winter and when the tonnage is heavy, upwards to eight diesels are used to get the train over the hill. *(Jim Shaughnessy)*

Freight #376 is about to enter the deep rock cut at the summit, known as the "Gateway," with solid rock walls over 50 feet in height. Old mountain fighter, Class S Mikado #616 is on the rear assisting the 683 and 682 up front in February of 1950. Behind the train, unfolds the panorama of the White Mountains of New Hampshire. *(Philip R. Hastings)*

Train #163 for Portland waits at Quebec Junction for the Beecher Falls local and a car of milk for Boston. Today, one of the stainless steel combines graces the rear. *(Herman Shaner)*

Old-time ball signals still guard the diamond crossing at Whitefield. The conductor of Maine Central's eastbound freight YR-1 has reset the signal and is ready to proceed as soon as the Boston & Maine freight clears in this 1961 scene. *(Donald S. Robinson)*

Photographer Roger P. Cook chanced upon a couple of freights at the Whitefield diamond on a late August afternoon in 1970. Maine Central's 561 with the Quebec Junction local clatters over the diamond on the return trip to St. Johnsbury, Vermont. The trailing steel caboose was remodeled from a boxcar. Boston & Maine freight UJ-2, below, from Berlin, approaches from the east with three GP-7s. The conductor has booked in, and after resetting the ball signal, they're off for White River Junction.

Train Time at Woodsville! The White River Junction local picks up a car of milk, then takes a break while passengers get on. *(470 Railroad Club)*

The local passenger train from Berlin whisks along the Ammonoosuc River at Bath on the line to Woodsville. A case for the "picture worth a thousand words." *(Jim Shaughnessy)*

Barre & Chelsea's westbound mixed train No. 3 is ready to leave Woodsville as soon as Boston & Maine's 1552, just in off Train #9 from Concord, clears the yard in June of 1950.

Canadian Pacific E-8 #1802 approaches the summit at Glencliff with southbound train #20, the "Alouette" on May 14, 1950. *(Both photos Philip R. Hastings)*

East Branch & Lincoln #1 sets a car of paper on the scale in the yards of parent company Franconia Paper Corp. at Lincoln in the summer of 1960. *(Walker Transportation Collection—Beverly Historical Society)*

Boston & Maine GP-7 1575 heads out of Lincoln with the local for Concord on August 25, 1964. *(Jack Swanberg)*

A northbound local rolls through a heavy autumn mist at Swainboro on the old Plymouth-Woodsville line on September 30, 1954, shortly before abandonment of this section. The 1551 with its distinctive lines truly exemplifies its builders designation, "Branch Line." *(Donald S. Robinson)*

Train #10, the Woodsville to Concord local, arrives at Plymouth with Diesel Railcar 1140 and two cars in August of 1951. *(470 Railroad Club)*

Boston & Maine's No. 5, the "Alouette," glides into the station at Plymouth behind Canadian Pacific E-8 #1801 in June of 1953. The southbound local freight, OC-2, waits in the hole for No. 5 to clear. *(Dwight A. Smith)*

The Concord local from Lincoln is just coming to a halt at Lakeport and the conductor and crew of 44 tonner #116 seem very intent on where the set-off will go; the conductor is pointing to the Lakeshore Branch in the foreground, a remnant of the line to Rochester. *(Herman Shaner)*

Here comes the Mountaineer! No. 6000, the former "Flying Yankee," wears a new name plate on the Boston to Littleton summer service. She has just left the Boston & Maine's Conway branch and is heading west over the Maine Central at Intervale in July 1938. Test runs were made on the Mountain Subdivision in 1936 in preparation for this run. *(Harold K. Vollrath)*

Boston & Maine RDC with the southbound connection for Boston, skirts the placid waters of Silver Lake near Madison on the Conway branch in June 1953. *(Jim Shaughnessy)*

Maine Central's #709 crosses the Connecticut River into Westboro, N.H. with the southbound "Ambassador" from Montreal on April 24, 1953. White River Junction and the Vermont hills form a scenic backdrop for the wandering E-7 from Maine. *(George C. Corey photo—Dave Albert collection)*

An F-2 A&B set leads Boston & Maine train #320 south at Canaan on the New Hampshire Division between White River Junction and Concord in February 1953. The photographer caught this scene from a northbound RDC in the siding for the meet. *(Wayne D. Allen collection)*

Brand-new Alco S-3 1182 passes the station at Contoocook on the Claremont branch with the local switching run from Concord in 1952. The shiny "intruder" signals the end of the last stronghold of Boston & Maine's classic Moguls. *(Dwight A. Smith)*

E-7 Interlude. The Sunday-only Train 407, a local to Plymouth sits under the trainshed at Concord in 1951 while waiting for the northbound Train 307, the Boston section of the "Ambassador," which has just arrived in the foreground. *(Walker Transportation Collection—Beverly Historical Society)*

Alco HH600 #1161, renumbered from 1101, switches the yard at Concord on April 9, 1953. Only four of this type showed up on the Boston & Maine roster. *(Dave Engman)*

On February 6, 1976, the new Wolfboro Railroad began operations over the former Boston & Maine White Mountain branch from Concord to Lincoln. The reopening of the paper mill at Lincoln resulted in the State of New Hampshire purchasing the 70 miles of track and leasing it to a private operator. No. 101, former Maine Central 557, is the lines only power. *(Alan Thomas)*

Claremont & Concord #18 places an oil car at the Claremont Papers facility in Claremont. Don't let that little truck throw you! The date is 1975 and not 1942! This line began operations in 1954 over the old Claremont branch of the Boston & Maine and a portion of the Claremont Railway electric line. *(George Melvin)*

No. 31, formerly of the Sanford & Eastern in Maine, ambles through the covered bridge over the Sugar River near Chandler with a fan trip for Newport on June 8, 1975. The 12 miles from Claremont to Newport are up for abandonment and this was one of the final trips over this segment. *(Ronald N. Johnson)*

A light snow dusts the 17 as a pick-up is made at Bradford in the late 1950's. Dwindling freight revenues forced the abandonment of the section from West Concord to Newport in 1962; thus severing the eastern connection with the Boston & Maine. *(Walker Transportation Collection—Beverly Historical Society)*

An eastbound train rattles past an old highway covered bridge at Waterloo in 1956. It seems that #11 is caught in a swirl of October leaves. *(Donald S. Robinson)*

When the Boston & Maine gave up its Suncook Valley branch from Suncook, on the Concord line, to Center Barnstead in 1927, a spirited band of shippers and townfolk were determined to have their own railroad. And they did; the Suncook Valley Railroad. After steamer #1 played out, a second-hand GE 45-tonner showed up and #2 is seen, above, arriving with the mixed train at Epsom on September 8, 1950. *(Norton D. Clark)*

New 44-tonner #3, acquired in 1951, approaches Allenstown in May 1952. The engineer has a friendly wave for the photographer's daughter Martha who seems not afraid. The former B&M baggage-RPO car on the rear still carried the mail and an occasional passenger. Abandonment unfortunately came on December 15, 1952. *(Dwight A. Smith)*

Rockingham Junction, N.H. on the Boston & Maine is where the Boston to Portland mainline crosses the Manchester to Portsmouth branch. In this 1952 scene, GP-7 #1564 on the Portsmouth local, above, is backing off the diamond for the passage of mainline tonnage in the form of Rigby-Mechanicville freight RM-3, below, with a quartet of FT's. *(Both photos Herman Shaner)*

A most unusual duo! A pair of new Alco RSD-7 demonstrators bring Boston & Maine freight BU-3 into Manchester on March 11, 1954. Apparently unsuccessful in making a sale in New England, they later went to the Santa Fe. *(Dwight A. Smith)*

New Haven's 0500 arrives in Manchester with the Portsmouth local in 1953. The Boston & Maine leased the 0500 along with 0501, 0504, 0512 and 0514 while awaiting the arrival of new SW-9's 1226-1231. The five New Haven units saw service on Central Mass branch and Salem locals and passenger runs to Lowell. *(Dave Engman)*

The pastoral village of Hillsboro in southwestern New Hampshire, served by a 44 mile branch from Nashua, once saw the daily comings and goings of Mogul-powered trains until 1954. Since the arrival of the diesel, however, the branch has lost none of its charm. Alan Thomas has recorded a couple of arrivals, as an Alco switcher rumbles over the trestle below the station and, below, an SW-1 struggles into town after a hard winter run. The covered bridge over the frozen Contoocook River is one of two on the line. Today, the branch is out of service and may never see the passage of trains again.

Boston & Maine's first RS-2 #1500 knocks new-fallen snow off a small bridge at East Jaffrey as it wends its way up the Peterboro branch in February 1963. The black "switcher" style paint was later replaced with the standard "B&M Blue." Damaged in a derailment in February 1975, the 1500 is now stored ending 26 years of service. *(Russ Munroe, Jr.)*

The local freight for Keene rambles through the summer countryside on the Ashuelot branch in August 1954. The brakeman rides the front pilot, ready to flag the crossing as they approach Winchester. With the old Chesire branch from Winchendon, Mass. through Keene to Bellows Falls, Vermont out of service, this line is the only rail connection to the city. *(Dave Engman)*

VERMONT

George Melvin

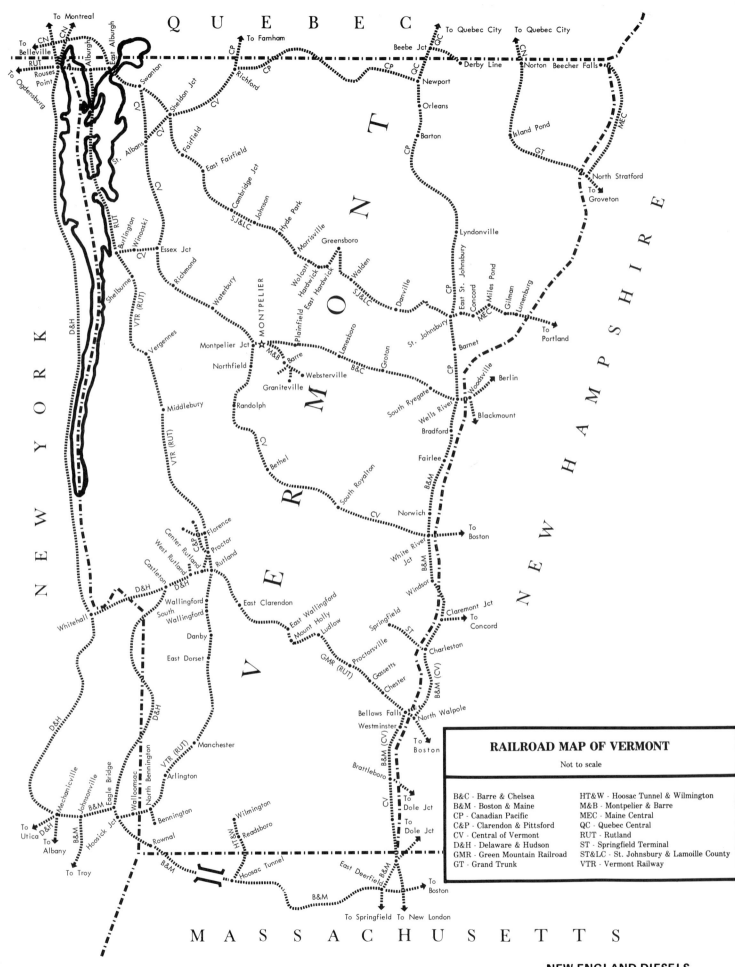

RAILROAD MAP OF VERMONT

Not to scale

B&C - Barre & Chelsea	HT&W - Hoosac Tunnel & Wilmington
B&M - Boston & Maine	M&B - Montpelier & Barre
CP - Canadian Pacific	MEC - Maine Central
C&P - Clarendon & Pittsford	QC - Quebec Central
CV - Central of Vermont	RUT - Rutland
D&H - Delaware & Hudson	ST - Springfield Terminal
GMR - Green Mountain Railroad	ST&LC - St. Johnsbury & Lamoille County
GT - Grand Trunk	VTR - Vermont Railway

NEW ENGLAND DIESELS

Northbound freight #19 roars out of Alburg for the New York Central connection at Norwood, New York on the old Rutland line in June 1951. A polished 201, fresh from the builder, assists veteran Mike #34. *(470 Railroad Club)*

Milk was a big plus on Rutland's balance sheet. The southbound milk train stands at Alburg station for orders in 1951. More cars will be added on the trip down the line. *(George C. Corey—Dave Albert collection)*

Canadian Pacific freight #904 smokes up a storm as they cross the Missisquoi River at Richford southbound for Newport on April 12, 1975. Four or five units on this train is not uncommon.

To the west on the same day, a pair of Central Vermont SW-1200's lead the Richford local over the Missisquoi River at Sheldon Junction where they interchange with the St. Johnsbury & Lamoille County R.R. *(Both photos Ronald N. Johnson)*

Roger Cook provides a look at the waning days of regular passenger service on the Central Vermont in August 1966. Above, the northbound "Montrealer" moves slowly across the wood pile trestle over Lake Champlain at East Alburg with two GP-9's and seven cars in tow, while down the line at Swanton, the 4927 grinds to a halt for its appointed stop with the northbound "Ambassador."

Like a one-eyed monster entering its cave, Central Vermont's southbound "Ambassador" rumbles into the cavernous trainshed at St. Albans in August 1963. The four-track shed had an ornate brick facade at either end and was attached to an equally classic brick station-general office building. *(Roger P. Cook)*

The revival of passenger service on the Central Vermont on September 29, 1972, came in the form of Amtrak's Washington-Montreal service. Here at St. Albans, E-9 units 263 and 260 pull the northbound Train #60, "Montrealer," away from the remains of the old depot on July 31, 1974. *(Philip R. Hastings)*

A mixture of black Central Vermont and Grand Trunk GP-9's on the southbound through freight for East New London, Connecticut get underway at Italy Yard in St. Albans in May 1971. The new extended vision caboose with the "picture windows" over to the right, is quite an improvement over "old 4018" pictured at right. (George Melvin)

Train #538, the daily turn job from St. Albans to Burlington, enters the tunnel leading to Burlington Bay on Lake Champlain on March 6, 1972. SW-1200 #1511 with the characteristic "four-barrel" exhaust stacks has the honors today. (Philip R. Hastings)

The Vermont Railway, operating over a portion of the old Rutland, began service in mid-winter of 1964 and immediately ran into snow problems. Here in March, the Burlington-Rutland freight with the plow up front, barrels over a frozen stream near Shelburne. The RS-1 and snow-caked plow are former Rutland equipment. *(Roger P. Cook)*

A decade has passed and the Vermont Railway has emerged as a thriving and prosperous shortline. At Burlington, the roads northern terminus and repair shop, the late-afternoon freight is ready for its southbound departure for Rutland on April 2, 1974. *(Frank DiFalco)*

New GE 70-ton diesels #46 and 47 haul westbound Train #75 down the scenic Lamoille River valley near Hyde Park in the summer of 1948. The new arrivals on the St. J. & L.C. have displaced the venerable B&M K-7 2-8-0's and now it's the sound of an air horn that echoes off Mt. Mansfield in the distance.

Engineer Marshall MacDonald is accelerating Central Vermont RS-3 #1860 away from a station stop with Train #332, the southbound "Ambassador." RS-3 #1859 is in the hole with the northbound milk train #211 in this March 1955 scene. *(Both photos Philip R. Hastings)*

St. J. & L.C. mixed train #51, trailing the usual milk cars ahead of the old combine, arrives at Morrisville on April 31, 1948. It is what's up front that is unusual. This is the first trip for #46 and the young ladies at the right are getting their first look at this new wonder. *(470 Railroad Club)*

In later years, after surviving two near-abandonments, the fleet of 70-tonners wore out and second-hand GP-9's and RS-3's showed up on the roster. The Morrisville-Swanton freight, with RS-3 #204 in charge, crosses the Black Creek near East Fairfield on August 19, 1975. *(Jack Armstrong)*

Rugged GE 70-tonners marked nearly two decades of service on the old St. J. Russ Munroe, Jr. lensed a pair of hard-working freights in 1963. Above, 54 leads a freight through the "Fisher" covered bridge east of Wolcott and, below, a trio on the eastbound freight rounds a curve near Danville on the long downgrade run into St. Johnsbury.

First Canadian Pacific diesels across the border! New Alco FA-1's arrive at Newport, Vermont with freight #904 on one of the first trips for the units in June 1949. The delivery, that year, of 8 FA-1's, 4 FB-1's, 5 RS-2's, 2 S-2's and 3 EMD E-8's saw complete dieselization of the Montreal-Wells River division. In this scene, the new diesels pass an old steam boat on Lake Memphremagog. *(Philip R. Hastings)*

Southbound freight #916 rounds the curve into Newport yard for a meet with northbound freight #903. RS-10 #8477's companions include Boston & Maine RS-3 #1507 on lease to the Canadian road. In the hole at left, FPA-2 #4096 is being assisted by a CPR RS-3, another B&M RS-3, and sister #4095. *(George Melvin)*

Crystal Lake at Barton, Vermont provides an excellent location for photographs as we see here . . .
. . . Polished RS-3 #8403 heads north with the St. Johnsbury-Newport local in October 1975. (Roger P. Cook)

. . . Freight #904 for White River Junction works south with a pair of RS-10's bracketing Boston & Maine F-7B #4265 in July 1971. (Scott Hartley)

The village of Island Pond in the remote northern reaches of Vermont was an important division point on the Grand Trunk. The summer-only passenger extra makes a stop here to complete the customs inspection which began north of the border. The unit behind the RS-11's is a steam generator car. Today, the station remains intact but most of the yard, engine terminal and the overhead footbridge are gone. Below, northbound freight #493 pounds toward the Canadian border above Island Pond in July 1964. *(Both photos Roger P. Cook)*

It is July of 1964 and the southbound "Alouette," now a single RDC, approaches the station at Lyndonville on the Canadian Pacific. *(Roger P. Cook)*

St. J.&L.C. Extra 201 East waits patiently for Canadian Pacific southbound freight #904 to complete its setting off and picking up chores before entering the yard at St. Johnsbury on August 28, 1968. The 201 is one of two former New York Central GP-9's and as for the Canadian quartet; the ubiquitous RS-18's. *(Philip R. Hastings)*

The St. J entered the era of "big time" railroading in the late 1960's with a revamped roster of five RS-3's and a pair of GP-9's. Tripleheaders were rare, but on occasion when business was good, a train often had 40 or more cars. The westbound freight is ready to depart St. Johnsbury with tonnage behind the 201, 204 and former Lehigh & Hudson River #10 in August 1972. *(George Melvin)*

Eastbound Maine Central freight RY-2 from Portland, having left the White Mountain range of New Hampshire behind it, coasts downgrade into East St. Johnsbury about a mile or two from the end of its run in February 1970. *(Jim Shaughnessy)*

An FPA-2 and FB-1 race along just below St. Johnsbury with the southbound freight for White River Junction in July 1964. (Roger P. Cook)

Framed in the rear door of the combine, Barre & Chelsea 70-tonner backs down the siding to pick up a milk car while working westbound Train #4 at Plainfield on July 4, 1949. (Philip R. Hastings)

Two-thirds of Barre & Chelsea's diesel roster is busy at the yard in Barre in May 1956. The granite hauling road dieselized in 1947 with three GE 70-ton switchers. No. 12 is on the "Hill" job serving the huge quarries at Graniteville and Websterville over 3 and 4 percent grades and several switchbacks. No. 14 is the Barre switcher and later in the day both will doublehead the mainline freight from Montpelier to Woodsville, N.H. and return. *(Dwight A. Smith)*

With the abandonment of the mainline in 1956, the Barre & Chelsea became the Montpelier & Barre, a Pinsly operation, serving only the quarries and local businesses in the area. Here, #28, a former Boston & Maine SW-1, has made the morning run up from Montpelier and the Central Vermont connection at Montpelier Junction on November 11, 1972. The crew is getting their switch list at the freight office, the old CV station, in Barre. *(George Melvin)*

Central Vermont freight #429 rolls through the scenic countryside at Royalton with a pair of Canadian National Fairbanks-Morse C-Liners, #8716 and 8726, on May 24, 1953. *(470 Railroad Club)*

Canadian Pacific train #212, the southbound "Alouette," swings onto Boston & Maine trackage at Wells River in February 1950. After its stop here, the Boston bound train will cross the Connecticut River into Woodsville, N.H. for its run over the White Mountains division mainline to Concord. The Barre & Chelsea line from Montpelier enters the yard just in front of the water tank. *(Philip R. Hastings)*

Southbound Canadian Pacific freight #904 arrives at Wells River station with two rush cars of meat on the head end to set off for a Boston & Maine connection in April 1954. Below, with the chores taken care of and a green signal ahead, FPA-2 #4098 and FA-1 #4001 are about to enter the Boston & Maine joint trackage for the run to White River Junction. *(Both photos Dwight A. Smith)*

Boston & Maine Sunday local passenger train #6051 approaches a rock cut at Stone Cliffs near Bradford in February 1950. This train is making a leisurely trip up to Lancaster, N.H. from White River Junction and return, and has a prime mission; the return of empty milk cars, four of which are seen in this consist. New Canadian Pacific E-8 #1800, which was laying over at White River Junction, is being used this day.

BL-2 #1552 leads southbound milk train, #48, across the Waits River at Bradford on May 14, 1950; back when a milk train was really that. *(Both photos Philip R. Hastings)*

The afternoon rush at White River Junction was always a drawing card for railfans and August 21, 1965 was no disappointment. The southbound "Ambassador" stands at the platform with F-7 #4268 on the point after being brought over from the Westboro, N.H. enginehouse by Central Vermont S-2 #8094, now drifting back to the CV yard, while F-7 #4266 comes down the Wells River mainline with Canadian Pacific freight #916 from Newport. *(George Melvin)*

The trackage is Boston & Maine, the train and crew is Canadian Pacific, and the power is mixed. Canadian Pacific train #904 (B&M 8904) approaches Norwich on August 6, 1974. *(Scott Hartley)*

The summer of 1958 still saw plenty of activity at the "Junction" as the Boston & Maine local from Woodsville, N.H. waits for a pair of Canadian Pacific RS-18's to clear the switch. The 8741 and 8771 are on their way to the Boston & Maine enginehouse across the Connecticut River in Westboro, N.H. *(Dave Engman)*

The Connecticut River mainline freights during the 1960's were handled primarily by Boston & Maine's dual service RS-3's after they were bumped from passenger runs by the RDC's. JS-4 hauls out of the south end of the White River Junction yard with a typical combination of RS-3, F-7B, and RS-3 on August 30, 1966. *(Frank DiFalco photo—Jay Potter collection)*

With two RS-11's reassigned from the Duluth, Winnepeg & Pacific in Minnesota, the northbound #430 from East New London, Connecticut hauls into the yard at White River Junction on August 21, 1965. *(George Melvin)*

Northbound freight JU-1 for Newport gets a push out of White River by Boston & Maine #1261, an Alco 1000 HP S-2, in July 1948. The train has a Canadian Pacific engine and caboose for the run over its own iron and the helper to the White River yard limit enables northbound freight to take 300 to 500 more tons for the run to Wells River. *(Philip R. Hastings)*

Springfield Terminal #1 crosses the Black River on the dual rail-highway bridge enroute from Charlestown, N.H. to Springfield, Vermont in 1974. The former electric line, owned by the Boston & Maine, dieselized in 1956 with this former Sacramento Northern (California) 44-tonner rebuilt by General Electric. *(Dave Albert)*

Former Rutland #500 heads a northbound train of marble and lime products on the 18 mile Clarendon & Pittsford at West Rutland on November 15, 1962. The GE 70-tonner was purchased in August of that year after the Rutland ceased operations and was later renumbered 12. *(Donald S. Robinson)*

Delaware & Hudson RS-2 #4005 has arrived at Center Rutland with the daily local from Whitehall, N.Y. and is busy with the switching chores in this 1947 scene. In the background, Clarendon & Pittsford's #11 waits to use the diamond. This was one of two interchange points with the marble road. *(Philip R. Hastings)*

Clarendon & Pittsford #10 breezes along the mainline with a 12 car train of marble. This road became the first Vermont railroad to dieselize in 1945 with the acquisition of two Whitcomb 44-tonners weighted down to 50 tons for greater tractive effort. After 87 years of operation by parent company, Vermont Marble, the line was sold to the Vermont Railway in November 1972. *(Walker Transportation Collection—Beverly Historical Society)*

The Green Mountain Railroad, which began operations in April 1965, operates over the Bellows Falls to Rutland segment of the old Rutland Railroad. Here, northbound freight XR-1 crests the grade on Mt. Holly near Healdsville on June 28, 1972. S-4 #303 came from the Delaware & Hudson and the trailing RS-1 #405 is a former Rutland engine. *(Jack Armstrong)*

The daily local, with the 303 in charge again, rolls across the Williams River near Gassetts in February 1972. *(Scott Hartley)*

Freight XR-1 passes through the village of East Wallingford on its run to Rutland in February 1966. The Green Mountain line is less than a year old in this scene, but it has survived 11 hard Vermont winters. *(Donald S. Robinson)*

Train time at Windsor! E-7 #3803 brings the Connecticut River line train to a halt at the station as the agent gets ready to hand up orders. The fellow to the left has his truck ready for the mail pick-up. The year is 1950. *(Walker Transportation Collection—Beverly Historical Society)*

Boston & Maine RS-3 #1545 has just brought Train 165 into Bellows Falls after a run over the Chesire branch in April 1953. The ball signal at the right protects the movements over the diamonds of the Connecticut River mainline which cuts across the yard in the foreground. A pair of Rutland RS-3's, 202 and 203, just in off a freight, wait on the service track for another assignment. *(470 Railroad Club)*

Southbound freight JE-2 rounds the curve at Westminster with Boston & Maine RS-3's 1539 and 1545 and a slug of milk cars on April 21, 1963. *(Neil D. Richardson)*

From out of the hills! Vermont Railway's #602 heads southbound freight RC-2 at South Wallingford on a misty April day in 1974. The train seems to be literally emerging from the enveloping green mountains. The Rutland-North Bennington section, called the Southern Subdivision, provides a vital link with the Boston & Maine. *(Dave Albert)*

In 1966, Vermont Railway purchased its first new diesel to assist the aging second-hand units on the roster and #501, an EMD SW1500, has proved its worth. Here at Mt. Tabor, she handles southbound RC-2 on the run to North Bennington in January 1975. *(Jack Armstrong)*

Although usually assigned to the Northern Subdivision out of Burlington, the new GP-38-2's occasionally find themselves assigned to the North Bennington turn. The 201 rolls five cars of RC-2 south of Danby on June 27, 1975. *(Ronald N. Johnson)*

The North Bennington yard can get busy when more than one train arrives in town. On a rainy afternoon in April 1974, Vermont Railway's 602 breaks up its train in the yard while Boston & Maine NW-2 #1204, just in with the local from Mechanicville, N.Y., comes up the west leg of the wye. *(Dave Albert)*

For a short period in 1975, a "strange" pair of RS-3's were seen at North Bennington on the local from Mechanicville. Formerly Delaware & Hudson #4075 and 4082, they went to the Providence & Worcester as #162 and 164, then to the Boston & Maine as #1508 and 1536 in a swap for the original B&M 1508 and 1536, thus giving the D&H additional boiler-equipped power for the "Adirondack" passenger service. They have since been leased back to the D&H and renumbered 4075 and 4082. Got that? *(Frank DiFalco)*

MASSACHUSETTS

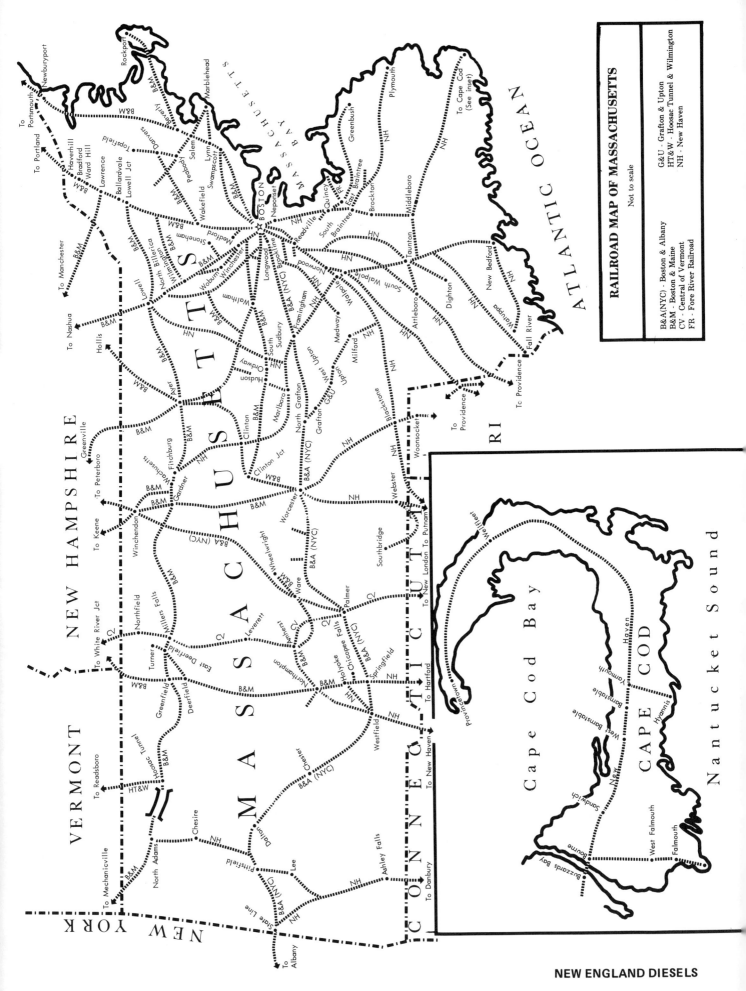

RAILROAD MAP OF MASSACHUSETTS

Not to scale

B&A(NYC) - Boston & Albany
B&M - Boston & Maine
CV - Central of Vermont
FR - Fore River Railroad

G&U - Grafton & Upton
HT&W - Hoosac Tunnel & Wilmington
NH - New Haven

ATLANTIC OCEAN

MASSACHUSETTS BAY

NEW HAMPSHIRE

VERMONT

NEW YORK

CONNECTICUT

RI

Cape Cod Bay

CAPE COD

Buzzards Bay

Nantucket Sound

NEW ENGLAND DIESELS

Local freight D-4, with S-2 1265, one of several repainted in the maroon roadswitcher colors, is working through Bradford in 1964 on its Dover, NH-Lowell turn around.

After the demise of through passenger service into Maine from Boston and Worcester, the NH-B&M-MEC operated summer passenger extras for summer camps in Maine. B&M GP-9 1743 is rolling through Ward Hill in the mid 1960's with a westbound deadhead move of empty Pullmans for Penn. Station in New York City. *(Both photos, Frank DiFalco)*

Photographer Stan Bolton recorded two afternoon locals at Ballardvale on May 9, 1953 providing a look at the endless parade of shiny maroon roadswitchers and coaches on the lines radiating out of Boston. GP-7 1575 is handling train 160, an inward (Boston-bound) Haverhill local.

RS-3 1543 wheels outward with Haverhill run 141. (Both photos, Dave Albert collection)

Despite the optimism over lightweight trains in the 1950's, their success was marginal and the Boston & Maine's FM-powered Talgo set, 1 and 2, spent most of its life hauling commuters on North Shore runs and is shown at Rockport in 1959. Today, the locomotives are standby power plants for a scrap company in Leeds, Maine. *(Walker Transportation Collection—Beverly Historical Society)*

The downtown section of Salem is spliced by the Boston & Maine's Eastern Route which operates through a tunnel. GP-7 1563 is lifting an inward local out of the tunnel and into Salem station in 1954. *(Russ Munroe, Jr.)*

Boston & Maine was the largest owner of Budd RDC's and used them to replace all conventional local trains and most long distance trains still running into the 1960's. A trio of RDC-1's pass the station-tower at Lowell Junction. *(Phil Faudi)*

In charge of local train #3006 storming through Lowell in 1951, is two-year old BL-2 #1552. Steam-generator equipped and lacking MU, these four units, 1550-1553, were bought for the Boston commuter pool in 1949. *(470 Railroad Club)*

Passing North Woburn Junction, FT set 4221 with train 309 is 12 miles from Boston on its 124 mile run to Plymouth, New Hampshire. It has plenty to do—ten regular stops and three flagstops and maintain a three-hour schedule to Plymouth! *(470 Railroad Club)*

Another New Hampshire Division scene is RS-3 1512, still brand new on October 23, 1954, with Lowell-bound local 3321 at Winchester. *(Stan Bolton photo—Dave Albert Collection)*

In the early maroon, yellow and silver scheme, E-7 3809 and a sister E-7 prepare to take a long train of heavyweight cars out of North Station in 1947. *(Photo courtesy of Maine Central Railroad)*

In the summer of 1946, the Boston & Maine had already invested in FT's and E-7's but was nevertheless testing an Electro-Motive F-2 in passenger service—on a foursome of open-platform wooden cars! *(Wayne D. Allen Collection)*

Portland Terminal GP-7 1081 arriving at North Station with local 214 from Portsmouth in 1955. *(Dave Albert collection)*

The total commitment to self-propelled passenger equipment by the 1960's is exemplified by Frank DiFalco's view in North Station on August 18, 1964 of CP RDC-2 9113 in from the Montreal pool run via White River Junction and Newport, the remaining remnant of the "Alouette," in company of B&M RDC's and the FM Talgo.

Although built four months after B&M's first diesel, HH600 1102, centercab 1100 of 1935 was most unique. Internally, it was primarily a boxcab locomotive, containing two three hundred horsepower Ingersoll-Rand 10X12 engines placed in a more modern hood type design. The Lackawanna was the only other buyer of this model. At East Somerville on October 16, 1949, the 1100 was scrapped one year later.

B&M SW-9 1228 and SW-8 805 stand at the Boston Hump Tower in Somerville, perhaps awaiting a crew change on April 26, 1969. *(Jay Potter)*

Alco power, old and new, wheel around the curves leaving South Station in 1956.

PA-1's with 0782 leading head a Passenger Extra running in advance of the "Yankee Clipper" which can be seen in the right background backing into the station and, below, blasting out of town with new RS-11's 1411 and 1400. Credit Herman Shaner with the fine lens work.

South Station saw a full spectrum of dieseldom in the early years.

New Haven's one of a kind "Comet," units 9200-9202 (in a motor-trailer-motor set), came in 1935 just after the "Flying Yankee." Powered by Westinghouse and billed by the New Haven as "A luxuriously comfortable new-type train," it was built for Boston-Providence service and made its final run in 1951. *(Russ Munroe, Jr.)*

One of New York Central's two A-B-A sets of Baldwin DR 6-4-15 "Babyface" passenger units thread through South Station's maze of slipswitches in July 1950. *(470 Railroad Club)*

Boston & Albany 684 is one of eleven Alco high hoods to originally carry Boston & Albany markings, never applied to any other model. At Beacon Park engine terminal in May, 1939: *(470 Railroad Club)*

Father of all high hoods, New Haven HH600 #0900 was handling one of its last assignments, work train duty on the South Shore line in Quincy in 1953. *(Stanley M. Hauck)*

In line with its pioneer dieselization, the New Haven was the largest owner of high hoods in New England; twenty-one units.

The 0917, in the early green scheme is an early model with the "feather-edge" hood. Shown working near Commonwealth Pier in Boston in 1950.

The 0929, a late model with the round edge hood and in the later "McGinnis" paint scheme, pushed cars under the Old Colony bridge on the Commonwealth Pier line in 1965. *(Both photos, Russ Munroe, Jr.)*

Union Freight 44-tonner 5 was one of five such MU-equipped centercabs to operate on the switching line along Atlantic Avenue in Boston. Bought new in 1946 but deemed too light and replaced by leased New Haven switchers in 1953, they were sold off and the five-spot worked for Vulcan Materials in Alabama until 1970. *(Russ Munroe, Jr.)*

Jay Potter caught this interesting scene between Dover Street engine terminal and coach yards and South Station soon after the New Haven-Penn Central merger. Renumbered New Haven GP-9 7543 is backing to the station with commuter equipment for an outward run while Penn Central E-8 4247 and renumbered New Haven FL-9 5034 in MU, back to the engine terminal after bringing a train in from New Haven.

Until early in 1972, three round-trips daily between Boston and Needham were handled by locomotive-hauled trains. Two of them were assigned RS-3's such as 5504 above at South Station on December 16, 1971. *(Scott Hartley)*

On November 29, 1975, the newly established "Lakeshore" leaves Boston for Albany with Amtrak SDP-40F 601 after four years without through service over the old Boston & Albany route. *(Frank DiFalco)*

New York Central PA's, led by 4210 bring the "New England States" through Back Bay station in 1950. (Russ Munroe, Jr.)

New Haven PA-1 0783 leads the "Yankee Clipper" at Back Bay in 1952. (Norton D. Clark)

It seems like *more* than twenty-five years have elapsed since these aristocrats were hauling travelers all over the nation. . .

Norton D. Clark made these two photographs of suburban trains in 1951 which provide us with a look at what are now nearly extinct models doing what they were built for—

. . . Baldwin DRS 4-4-15 7300 with five cars at Longwood station in Brookline and

. . . Lima 1200 HP roadswitcher 5805 and a single coach at Concord Street in Newton Lower Falls.

Readville was the site of major carshops for the New Haven and a junction with the Shore Line main and branches to Blackstone and Dedham.

Freshly painted H16-44 591 and a local on the Blackstone line at Readville in 1957.

44-tonner 0809 switches Readville Yard on the Dedham line in 1954. *(Stanley M. Hauck photos)*

New Haven H16-44 1600 stops at Neponset station on the final day of service on the Old Colony line in the summer of 1959. This spot is now Atlantic station on the Massachusetts Bay Transit Authority. *(Russ Munroe, Jr.)*

General Dynamics-owned switching road, the Fore River Railroad operates two and one half miles between Quincy and East Braintree. Unit 16 is one of two rare 1941 GE centercab 70-tonners making up their roster. *(Ronald N. Johnson)*

New Haven DL-109's 0718 and 0713 are laying over at Greenbush for morning commuter runs to South Station over the Old Colony line. *(Joseph Ryan Collection)*

After working a "boat train" to Woods Hole to connect with ferries for Martha's Vineyard and Nantucket summer retreats, FL-9's lay over in the yard in August 1962. *(Walker Transportation Collection—Beverly Historical Society)*

Ingersoll-Rand railcar 1140 with two cars trailing make up Central Mass. line local 3112 Boston-bound at Ordway. Train 3112 started its run at Lowell, deadheading south on the Worcester line to Clinton then turning eastward on the Central Mass. February 26, 1957. *(Donald S. Robinson)*

New Haven RDC-1 44 makes its appointed stop at Walpole on the Blackstone line in a scene duplicated many times throughout the New Haven's commuter territory. *(Walker Transportation Collection—Beverly Historical Society)*

The "Roger Williams," the custom built RDC with the FM-style nose was the only product of the lightweight train craze to enjoy any success and is still in service. Shown here leaving Attleboro in the late 1960's. *(Jay Potter)*

A trio of New Haven RS-2's leave Brockton in 1965 with the fifty-car James Strates Show bound for Framingham and the New York Central interchange. It will be an all day run as it must run south to Middleboro then through Taunton, crossing the Shore Line at Mansfield, then northward to Framingham. *(Russ Munroe, Jr.)*

The Grafton & Upton operates fifteen miles of former interurban trackage from a New Haven connection at Milford westward to a Boston & Albany connection at North Grafton. Now, both interchanges are Penn Central! The local for North Grafton works through West Upton in the early 1950's with 70-tonner #12. The 12 left the roster in 1954, leaving two 44-tonners, 10 and 11, and Alco S-4 #1001 remaining. *(Norton D. Clark)*

The daily freight rounds a curve near Upton in 1959 with #1001 and #10. *(Russ Munroe, Jr.)*

F-7's 4267A, 4267B and 4268B at Fitchburg in 1951 provide a look at Boston & Maine's last order of EMD F units for a total of eighty-one ordered! *(470 Railroad Club)*

A trio of Boston & Maine's GP-38-2's led by Bi Centennial unit 200 lead pool train NE-84 into Ayer in 1975. *(Frank DiFalco)*

A bit off their Boston to Bangor pool service, Maine Central E-7's 708 and 709 have teamed up to handle Train 54 from Troy, N.Y. to Boston on September 29, 1951. The train rolls eastward through the pretty countryside near Wachusett on the Fitchburg Division. *(Stan Bolton photo—Dave Albert Collection)*

Somewhere on the Fitchburg Division, the 6000 is operating as "The Minuteman," the last name it wore prior to retirement in 1956. *(Dave Albert Collection)*

Westbound freight PM-1 is cresting the grade at Gardner and is about to cut off the pusher it acquired at East Fitchburg for the run up the hill through South Ashburnham. It's downgrade now to Greenfield . . . then the Berkshires. *(Wayne D. Allen Collection)*

"East Wind," "Bar Harbor" . . . "State of Maine" were all familiar names at ticket windows everywhere. Carrying full equipment, these trains operated by the MEC-B&M-New Haven via Worcester between Maine points and the cities of the East.

New Haven DL-109 0717 is coupling onto New Haven train 193, the southbound "East Wind," just brought in from Portland by Boston & Maine E-7 3818, below, which has been turned and is heading B&M train 91, the northbound "East Wind" on August 14, 1949. (Both photos, Philip R. Hastings)

Maine Central also pooled power on the Worcester runs from Portland and Maine Central F-3 672A&B ride the Boston & Maine turntable after bringing B&M train 82, the overnight "State of Maine." (Philip R. Hastings)

New York Central FA-1's 1026 and 1025 speed westbound tonnage through Worcester on the Boston & Albany line in 1948. (Robert Baker, Sr.)

Providence & Worcester M-420 2002 rolls into the south end of Worcester yard with the local from Slatersville and Woonsocket. *(Alan Thomas)*

New Haven RS-11 1409 powers local BX-36 into Southbridge in June 1965. With its terminal at Worcester, this crew worked the Webster-Southbridge branch and the New London line as far as Putnam. 1976 may see the Providence & Worcester in charge of this trackage. *(D. A. Woodworth, Jr.)*

At Palmer, the Central Vermont's line to New London crosses the Boston & Albany line. In this 1951 view, New York Central RS-1 8102 clanks over the diamond enroute to Springfield while the southbound Central Vermont wayfreight with 2-8-0 467 waits her turn. *(Philip R. Hastings)*

Twenty-one years later, Palmer hosts Amtrak 448, the eastbound "Lakeshore Limited" with SDP-40F 593, making even the RS-1 above look ancient! *(Scott Hartley)*

Dieselization came late on the Canadian National's New England lines.

On January 24, 1956 Central Vermont freight 430 at Leverett has a pair of Canadian National F-3's and dynamometer car 69 establishing tonnage ratings for the GP-9's abuilding at LaGrange.

A month later, 2-8-0- 461, helper on freight 430 stands in the siding at Amherst for the passage of northbound freight 491 with Canadian National F-7's. Credit Dan Foley with these timely photographs.

Central Vermont southbound Brattleboro, Vermont-Palmer wayfreight with Grand Trunk GP-9 4442 just crossed the Vermont-Massachusetts line at Mount Herman, Mass. on June 1, 1974. *(Dave Albert)*

Jack Swanberg shot this Central Vermont freight running beside the Boston & Maine mainline at Millers Falls in 1967 without a Central Vermont unit in the combo! Grand Trunk GP-9's 4902, 4904 and 4449 lead Duluth Winnipeg & Pacific RS-11 3611.

Action at Greenfield station: E-7 3819 is on Troy-Boston day train 54 while the caboose belongs to a westbound freight for Mechanicville, New York. On the north side of the station, an RS-3 with local 716 loads passengers for Springfield. The date is June 24, 1954. *(Wayne D. Allen Collection)*

Photographer Frank DiFalco gets a tip of the cap from the brakeman on F-3 4228 leading two RS-3's between East Deerfield yard and Greenfield on a Connecticut River line freight.

Boston & Maine SW-1 1127 is one of fourteen such units built in 1953 for light branches. The 1127 is backing the Turners Falls local over its namesake branch in June 1975 *(Jack Armstrong)*

The Boston & Maine and Canadian Pacific power pool between Newport and White River Junction was extended to Springfield in the early 1970's. Northbound SJ-1, Springfield-White River Junction freight swings through Deerfield Junction on September 6, 1974 with a trio of Canadian Pacific RS-18's. *(Jack Armstrong)*

New Haven owned ten of the twenty-two F-M CPA 24-5 model 2400 HP "Super C-liners" built. Bought in 1950 and 1952, they lasted barely ten years on the road. Unit 798 is leaving Springfield in April 1957 wearing the new colors. *(Harvey D. Allen photo, Joe Snopek Collection)*

New Haven's thirty GP-9's gradually shifted from passenger to freight duties as passenger runs dwindled. On March 5, 1969, two months after the Penn Central merger, a pair prepares to take a freight to Cedar Hill from Springfield. *(Scott Hartley)*

Still lettered New York Central, Penn Central S-2 9634 switches the rider coach and Flexi-Vans from an eastbound mail train at Springfield station in February 1968. *(Scott Hartley)*

Six thousand first generation horsepower in the form of an A-B-B-A F-3 set in original colors handle a freight at Chester in the Berkshires in 1946. *(470 Railroad Club)*

Sparkling E-8's 4053 and 4066 rush westbound train 33, the "New England Wolverine" upgrade in the Berkshires Hills near Chester in July 1954.

Another pair of E-8's stride into the sunset with train 11, the "Southwestern Limited". *(Both photos, Philip R. Hastings)*

The hills loom close at Hoosac Tunnel station where the Deerfield River forms a narrow valley near the east portal of Hoosac Tunnel. Alco S-4 1270, above, is westbound crossing the Deerfield River headed for the big bore. *(Wayne D. Allen Collection)*

Hoosac Tunnel & Wilmington No. 16, a GE 44 tonner, is busy switching out cars at the paper mill of the Deerfield Glassine Co. in Monroe Bridge in the summer of 1962. This boomer diesel began life as D&RGW 39, then went to the Sanford & Eastern in Maine as their 14 and finally arrived on the HT&W in 1960. Nestled in the Berkshire hills along the Deerfield River valley, the 11 mile Pinsly-owned shortline ran from a Boston & Maine connection at Hoosac Tunnel to Readsboro, Vermont. The line was abandoned in 1972. *(Edward A. Lewis)*

Boston & Maine "low-nose" GP-18 #1750 leads GP-9's upgrade through the Berkshire Mountains near the Hoosac Tunnel in 1965. Six of these units, delivered to the Boston & Maine in 1961, arrived inadvertently numbered 1770-1775 and were immediately changed to 1750-1755. *(Russ Munroe, Jr.)*

New GP-38-2's #212, 207, and 205 power westbound freight NE-87 at Hoosac Tunnel in March 1974. The dozen units purchased in late 1973, represent the first new power since the GP-18's. *(Jack Armstrong)*

What do we have here! New York Central E-8 with the westbound "New England States" in tow, emerges from the west portal of the Hoosac Tunnel in an unscheduled appearance on the Boston & Maine. A washout on the Boston & Albany mainline on October 9, 1955 resulted in the re-routing of trains over the Fitchburg Division. *(Jim Shaughnessy)*

Heavy with head-end business, Boston-Troy, N.Y. locals pass at North Adams Junction on October 11, 1954. Eastbound Train #54 holds the siding with FT set #4222 while westbound Train #51 is headed by #3811 flying white flags. *(Donald S. Robinson)*

Rounding a curve along the Deerfield River at Charlemont in May 1974, is the New Hampshire Public Service unit coal train of empties from Bow, New Hampshire. Up front are two Penn Central U-30B's and Boston & Maine GP-9 #1738. *(Jack Armstrong)*

Jack Armstrong provides two New York Central scenes at Pittsfield in 1968. Freight BB-1 with an FA-2/FB-2 combo is deadheading an Alco switcher westward.

Penn Central train 428, the "New England States" stops amid winter activities as Penn Central RS-3 5336 prepares to take the snowplow at left up the North Adams Branch.

Today's action over the Boston & Albany line is a parade of second generation hoods; six motor U-Boats grind upgrade through Dalton in October 1975. *(Jack Armstrong)*

From Grand Central Terminal to an "Arm-strong" turntable in four hours, forty-two minutes! Sunday-only train 138 complete with a parlor car arrived at Pittsfield beside the turntable FL-9 2014 will use before returning to Grand Central with train 147, "The Litchfield." *(Jack Swanberg)*

Branch line stereotype! New Haven's Housatonic branch local grinds into the weed-covered yard at Lee past the neat wooden station of unusual architecture. *(Alan Thomas)*

Penn Central RS-2 #5229 was the huge system's last of this type in service and was retired early in 1975. It spent its final years on lines in western Massachusetts and is shown here at Ashley Falls on the Housatonic branch on October 18, 1974. *(Jack Armstrong)*

The twenty-mile branch from Pittsfield to North Adams is a complete contrast to Penn Central's big-time image. Penn Central SW-1500 9554 is working the northbound local along Hoosic Lake at Cheshire in 1974. *(Jack Armstrong)*

For seven miles, the Boston & Maine's line to Mechanicville slices through the southwestern corner of Vermont, following the Hoosic River. A trio of GP-38-2's wheel TC-100 toward Boston at North Pownal, Vermont on September 17, 1974. *(Jack Armstrong)*

CONNECTICUT

Joseph Ryan Collection

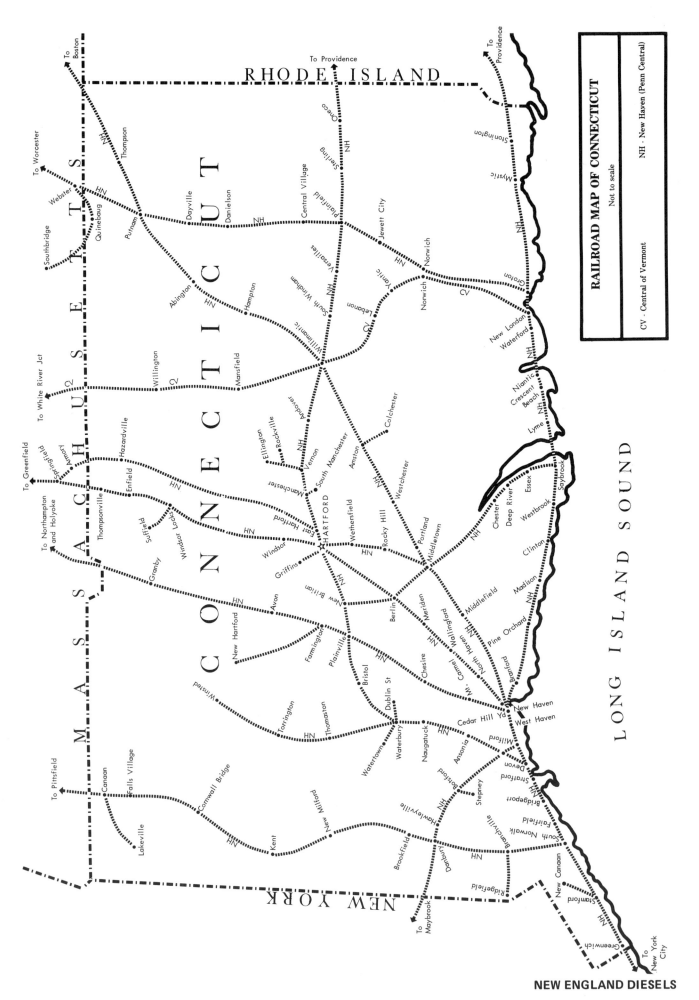

RAILROAD MAP OF CONNECTICUT
Not to scale

CV - Central of Vermont

NH - New Haven (Penn Central)

RHODE ISLAND

LONG ISLAND SOUND

NEW ENGLAND DIESELS

New Haven RS-3 520 switches at New London on December 24, 1965. The 520 is one of four RS-3's rebuilt by Alco in January 1962, as evidenced by the twin sealed-beam headlight applied during the rebuilding. *(D. A. Woodworth, Jr. Collection)*

Central Vermont GP-9 4925 takes the Yantic wayfreight north out of the road's southern terminus at East New London in April 1970. At the right is the Thames River pier of the United States Coast Guard Academy. *(Robert Redden)*

With the Alcos succeeded by the FL-9's during the New Haven era, the FL-9's in turn were replaced by E-8's under Penn Central and Amtrak control, the Shore Line main now is exemplified by these photos.

Penn Central E-8 4254 wheels the New York-Boston "Narragansett" through Old Saybrook in 1972 with a former Northern Pacific "Holiday Lounge" car in the consist. *(Scott Hartley)*

The New York-bound "Statesman" with Amtrak E-8 301 leading is passing bathers at Rocky Neck State Park near Niantic on June 6, 1975. *(Ronald N. Johnson)*

Action at Niantic! A pair of E-8's pass the abandoned freight house with an eastbound Amtrak run in the summer of 1972.

The Long Island Sound fog is still thick on this June 1968 morning as RS-3 547 with local BX-33 stays in the clear for the passage of symbol freight KN-1 on its South Braintree, Mass.-Cedar Hill Yard run. *(Scott Hartley photos)*

Local NX-20 is returning to Willimantic after working the stub branch to Abington and Pomfret, once part of the famous "Air Line" to Boston, which connected with the Norwich & Worcester line at Putnam until a flood in 1955 washed out a bridge at Putnam over the Quinebaug River. *(D. A. Woodworth, Jr.)*

Old Loewy-style H16-44 599 rolls a local over the diamond at Plainfield; a junction of the Worcester-New London mainline and the branch from Willimantic to Providence. *(Alan Thomas)*

176

A set of nearly-new FA-1's smoke through Putnam with a through freight in the 1950's. *(Russ Munroe, Jr.)*

During the 1950's "circle" fantrips out of South Station to Hartford, New Haven and return via the various branches were popular. Russ Munroe, Jr. photographed this one in 1953 with DL-109 0722, "The Cranberry" on the point. The 0722 was the only unit to carry this special bright red and white scheme.

A Penn Central RS-11 switches near the Willimantic-Columbia town line while on the local freight in December 1972. This trackage is the former Hartford to Willimantic line of the old New Haven and is abandoned between here and Manchester, a distance of 21 miles. *(Scott Hartley)*

All Connecticut is not suburban: With Grand Trunk GP-9 #4903, a wayfreight waits for orders at the small frame station in rural Lebanon on a rainy April morning. *(Robert Redden)*

Tomasso, Inc., formerly the New Haven Trap Rock Co., operates a six mile private line between North Branford and Pine Orchard serving its stone quarry and PC interchange and barge loading facility on Long Island Sound. Known as the Branford Steam RR (it operated steam until 1962) it uses four second-hand 44-tonners for its frequent hopper trains. Unit 4, above, is formerly Minneapolis & St. Louis D-149. Still in Hampton & Branchville colors, unit 6, below, switches at North Branford. Both photos taken October 13, 1972 by Edward F. DeVito.

New Haven DL-109 0743 wheels the fifteen standard cars of Train 79 along the Springfield line near Windsor in July 1948. *(Warren G. Fancher photo, New Haven Railroad Technical Information Assn.)*

Scott Hartley captured the passage of northbound mail train 16 at Enfield on January 25, 1973 with U-25B 2669 and Flexi-Vans. The New Haven was an early supporter of the piggyback concept and it seems fitting for this train to be on the New Haven.

Midday local 71 makes its first stop after leaving Springfield for New York at Thompsonville, April 25, 1968. Lead unit, H16-44 1609 was the only unit of the 1956 roadswitcher deliveries (GP-9's, RS-11's and H16-44's) to be repainted in the simplified orange and black scheme common on RS-3's in the 1960's.

Penn Central SW-1500 9548 working the Armory Branch local out of Springfield passes a steam era monument at Hazardville in 1973. *(Both photos, Scott Hartley)*

In the shadow of the state capitol, Hartford's station has seen years of New Haven passenger service. From 1948, when the DL-109's above rolled their consist around the curve into the station going south, until 1963 when FL-9 2056 performed the same task with a smaller lightweight train, only the equipment had changed and the vegetation gotten a firmer grip. *(Above, 470 Club Collection; below, George Melvin photo)*

Year -old H16-44 1600 stops northbound at Hartford station in September 1957. *(Jack Swanberg)*

A fourteen year old with a camera had attracted the attention of the crew of S-1 0978 working a local over Hamilton Street in Hartford in 1962. Moments later, the fourteen year old was on the brakeman's seat of the 0978 clanking down the mainline for a short ride! I never regretted the walk back . . . *(George Melvin)*

In 1956 and 1957, New Haven bought three variations of lightweight trains: the Budd RDC-based "Roger Williams," the Baldwin-powered "Dan'l Webster" with cars by Pullman and the Fairbanks-Morse powered "John Quincy Adams" which had ACF-built cars. The latter two were troublesome from the start and proved less endearing than the Revolutionary patriots they were named for; by the early 1960's, they were stored at Cedar Hill.

The "Dan'l Webster" sweeps around a curve on the Shore Line. *(Joe Ryan Collection)*

The "John Quincy Adams" is operating as train 14, the eastbound "Bostonian" at New Haven on April 14, 1957. *(Donald S. Robinson)*

Along with its investment in Alco High Hoods, the New Haven also bought ten "pre-standard era" switchers from General Electric, units 0901-0905 had Cooper-Bessemer diesel engines while units 0906-0910 had Ingersoll-Rand engines. The former units were sold to the Bangor & Aroostook in 1953; the 0903, shown switching New Haven station in 1940 became Bangor & Aroostook 32. *(Walker Transportation Collection—Beverly Historical Society)*

Jay Potter found this variety of power at the shop in New Haven on March 20, 1975; Amtrak E-9 432 in fresh paint PC GP-9 7530, Amtrak E-8 285, still in black, and PC SW-1500 9549.

FL-9's 2008 and 2003 depart New Haven for New York City on May 3, 1959 as an EP-4 electric idles to the shop at left. *(Jack Swanberg)*

Sunday, August 25, 1974 finds commuter power (Penn Central FL-9's in blue/yellow New York MTA colors) and Amtrak GG-1's laying over for Monday morning runs. "Cosmopolitan" M.U. cars have since replaced nearly all locomotive hauled commuter trains into New Haven. *(Scott Hartley)*

The only power bought by the New Haven in the 1960's came in the form of twenty-five U-25B's and ten C-425's in 1964. Two of the U-Boats with a Century trailing roll through West Haven under the wires with a Cedar Hill-Maybrook run on September 14, 1966. *(Jack Swanberg)*

SW-1200 650 performs flat switching at the south end of Cedar Hill Yard in 1968. This and the Cedar Hill Hump were normal assignments for the twenty Flexi-coil truck equipped units bought by the New Haven in 1956; their last switcher purchase. *(Scott Hartley)*

Derby Junction is the junction of the Maybrook mainline and the branch north to Waterbury and Torrington.

Acting as the Derby Switcher, S-1 0968 is retreiving cars left at Turkey Brook yard left by Cedar Hill-Waterbury freight ND-2.

Four FA-1's in three different paint schemes cross the Naugatuck River at Derby with Maybrook-bound NO-9. *(D. A. Woodworth, Jr. photos)*

What was double-track with automatic block signals and Alco cab units in the 1950's gave way to single track CTC and hood units in the 1960's. Jack Swanberg views at Hawleyville in 1957, above . . . and 1965, below, illustrate the change.

After a snowstorm, the New Haven considered an RDC too light for "breaking trail" up the branch north of Danbury. On December 28, 1969, renumbered GP-9 7548 is the "helper" for one of New Haven's two RDC-2's on train 138 at Danbury. *(Dan Foley)*

A fine sight! A trio of orange and green RS-3's power northbound symbol freight RI-2 through Danbury in late 1957 destined for State Line, Massachusetts and a New York Central connection. *(Jack Swanberg)*

Tugboat strikes in New York Harbor in the 1950's caused a rush of detour traffic through Maybrook and down the New Haven to Brooklyn and Long Island deliveries. Power borrowed to haul this tonnage was varied, ranging from Pennsy Sharks to Lackawanna F's and RS-3's! This westbound detour train has a quartet of Boston & Maine units at Danbury on June 21, 1959.

Usually assigned West of New Haven, the SW-1200's are still found on the New Haven region of the Penn Central. Here, unit 654 has a short local in tow at Danbury. *(Both photos, Jack Swanberg)*

FA-1's 0407 and 0429 forward eastbound tonnage over the Housatonic River at Devon on July 3, 1962. During this period, all New Haven freight electrics had been retired and the ex-Virginian rectifier units had not arrived, all freight service to New York was diesel-powered.

A four unit combo consisting of H16-44/RS-11/GP-9/RS-3, brings an eastbound Maybrook train into Devon on July 3, 1962. *(Both photos, Jack Swanberg)*

Scott Hartley is credited with these two views of activity at Devon on the morning of November 22, 1972: Above, Penn Central GP-40 3209 leads other EMD hoods through the switches leading to the Maybrook line. This Cedar Hill-Selkirk freight will not see Maybrook but will run to Hopewell Junction, down the branch to Beacon, New York and up the ex-New York Central Hudson line. Below, under the employ of the New York MTA, FL-9 5024 trundles commuters past the tower with ex-New York Central and ex-New Haven coaches in tow.

A "running meet" is captured by Dan Foley at Stratford in March 1966 as freight HN-2 with H16-44 1614 leading passes S-1 0948 with a local bound for East Bridgeport.

Although sold to the Youghiogheny & Ohio Coal Company in December, 1958 New Haven 44-tonner 0802 was never repainted and is shown switching in New Haven colors at Y&O Coal Co. in Stratford in 1962 where it remained until sold to a dealer in 1971. (D. A. Woodworth, Jr.)

RHODE ISLAND

Scott Hartley

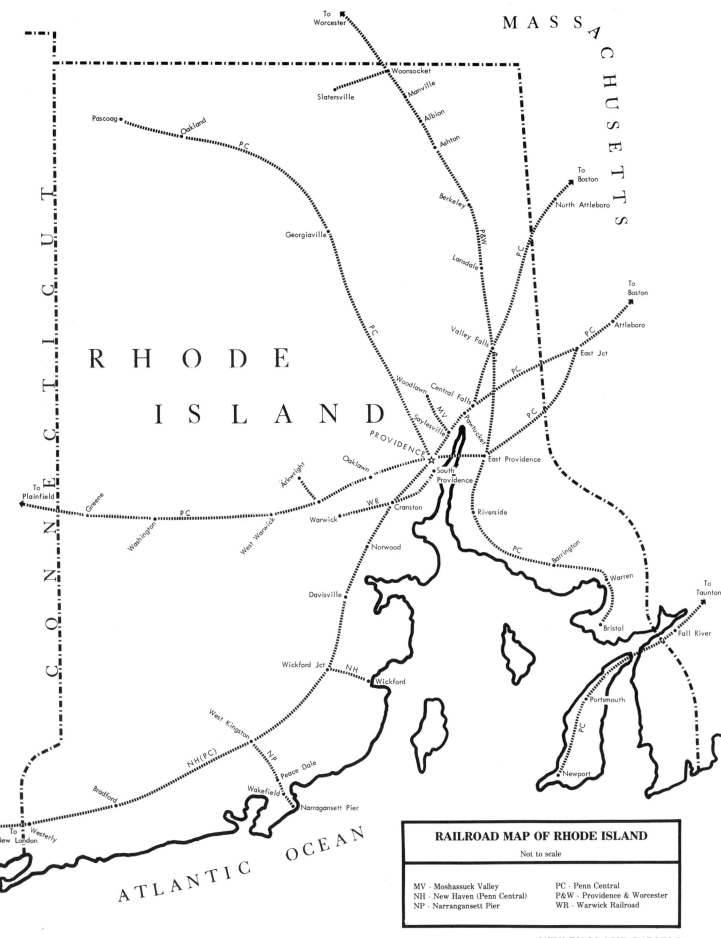

M A S S A C H U S E T T S

To Worcester

Woonsocket

Manville

Slatersville

Albion

Ashton

Pascoag

Oakland

PC

Berkeley

To Boston

North Attleboro

Georgiaville

P&W

PC

Lansdale

To Boston

R H O D E

I S L A N D

PC

PC

Attleboro

East Jct

PC

PC

Woodlawn

Central Falls

MV

Saylesville

Pawtucket

PC

PROVIDENCE

To Plainfield

Greene

Washington

Arkwright

Oaklawn

South Providence

East Providence

PC

West Warwick

W.R.

Cranston

Warwick

Riverside

Norwood

PC

Barrington

Davisville

Warren

To Taunton

Bristol

Fall River

Wickford Jct

NH

Wickford

Portsmouth

West Kingston

PC

NH(PC)

NP

Peace Dale

Bradford

Wakefield

Newport

To New London

Westerly

Narragansett Pier

A T L A N T I C   O C E A N

C O N N E C T I C U T

RAILROAD MAP OF RHODE ISLAND	
Not to scale	
MV - Moshassuck Valley	PC - Penn Central
NH - New Haven (Penn Central)	P&W - Providence & Worcester
NP - Narragansett Pier	WR - Warwick Railroad

NEW ENGLAND DIESELS

In the handsome hunter green scheme, five year old CPA 24-5 leads a PA-1 over the Rhode Island-Connecticut line near Central Falls in 1957. *(D. A. Woodworth, Jr.)*

After the delivery of the first two M-420's, the Providence & Worcester still had three D&H RS-3's on lease, making this combo possible. RS-3 165 and M-420 2002 are at Central Falls. *(Alan Thomas)*

M-420 2001 handles the north-bound through freight for Worcester and Gardner, Mass. through Albion late one afternoon. There are no turning facilities at the terminal in Valley Falls and crews prefer the engines facing south for the local freights so the 2001 must back to Worcester.

RS-3 164, below, switches at Woonsocket where the Providence & Worcester connects with the Slatersville Branch, a four mile isolated line of the Penn Central. Not part of the original P&W, this line is operated by P&W under agreement with the PC. *(Alan Thomas photos)*

Generally two locals crews work out of Valley Falls, one referred to as the "Berkley Job." Above, at Ashton, handles business north of Valley Falls towards the Massachusetts border. The other, the "East Providence Job," below, at Valley Falls, does the work south of Valley Falls. The Providence & Worcester M-420's 2001-2002 are the first MLW units sold in this country and now there are a total of five M-420's on the P&W, units 2001-2005. *(Frank DiFalco photos)*

P&W RS-3 164 works a long cut along the Industrial Highway in East Providence, a heavy revenue-producing area for the P&W. Photo taken in February, 1973, the first month of operation. *(George Melvin)*

The suburbs north of Providence are also industrial in nature and the home of the two-mile Moshassuck Valley Railroad. On April 21, 1975 Ronald N. Johnson found GE 65-tonner 9 returning from the Penn Central connection at Woodlawn to switch the industrial park at Sayleville, the little road's headquarters.

April 24, 1971 found Alcos of different ancestry on duty in East Providence.

Ex Pennsy RSD-15 6811 shuffles through the classification yard while assigned to the hump job.

Ex New Haven RS-11 7670 leads two new GP-38-2's on an eastbound freight. *(Both photos, George Melvin)*

Of the New Haven's twelve RS-1's, two units lasted into the 1970's as Penn Central 9944 and 9945. In April 1972, the 9945 idles between chores near the state capitol in Providence. *(Scott Hartley)*

The entire roster of the Warwick Railway is shown in this photo by Ronald N. Johnson. From left to right: Vulcan 65-ton 105, built in 1943, Atlas 104 (doing the chores this day) and 1924 GE gas-electric 101.

The "East Wind" name lives on as Amtrak train 168, passes the station at Kingston on June 3, 1974. Activity around station is caused by civic-sponsored renovation project. Note twin steam generators in these former Pennsylvania E-8's.

A relettered New Haven GP-9 passes the Kingston tower with a Providence-bound freight. *(Jay Potter photos)*

Jay Potter found a signal bridge a perfect frame for Penn Central RDC-1 72 near Kingston in February 1975. This car is still carrying the New Haven name on its letterboard in this view!

Narragansett Pier RR unit 40, an ex Navy Vulcan is at Peace Dale in June 1971. *(Norton D. Clark)*

NEW ENGLAND NEIGHBORS

To the north, south, east and west, New England's borders are crossed by neighboring roads that form the vital "gateways" for incoming products and outgoing tonnage for the western markets. Here are some scenes on the Canadian Pacific, Delaware and Hudson and some of our own roads that cross lines . . . Boston and Maine to Mechanicville and the New Haven to Maybrook.

With four Maine Central and four Canadian Pacific boxcars for a train, the St. Stephens wayfreight waits behind McAdam, New Brunswick's beautiful station, patterned after the Canadian Pacific station in Banff, Alberta. RS-23 8033 is bound for the St. Stephens and St. Andrews branches and will interchange with the Maine Central at Milltown Jct near Calais, Maine. *(Dave Albert)*

The June 30th, 1956 run of Canadian Pacific train #114, the Boston-St. John, New Brunswick "The Gull" shown leaving Fredericton Junction has Maine Central E-7 711 usually swapped at Vanceboro for a Pacific. *(Kenneth S. MacDonald)*

Woodstock, New Brunswick is a junction across the border from Houlton, Maine on the Canadian Pacific's McAdam-Aroostook, New Brunswick line. Russ Munroe, Jr., shows RS-3 8437 switching express cars onto its southbound tonnage in 1959.

With five MLW units maintaining the 50 MPH speed limit, transcon freight #949 hurries its containers west through the green and white winter landscape of Nantes, Quebec, just west of the crew change point at Megantic, Quebec where Maine-based crews gave the train over to Quebec-based crews. *(George Melvin)*

Making its last leg into Montreal's Windsor Station in 1950, Boston & Maine E-7 3817 speeds the overnight Boston-Montreal "Red Wing" out of Montreal West, Quebec. *(Harold K. Vollrath Collection)*

Rouses Point lies in the extreme northeast corner of New York State, on the Canadian and Vermont borders and is the "north end" on the Delaware & Hudson. RS-2M 4003 is using sand to start its southbound local out of the yard and past the station in this Alan Thomas view.

Could the Delaware & Hudson be mentioned without thinking of the PA's? Jim Shaughnessy shot PA-1 19 with the southbound "Laurentian" at Port Henry in 1968.

Train WR-1 (Wilkes-Barre to Rouses Point) runs the length of the D&H. Here, at Ticonderoga, New York in March 1976 WR-1 is powered by four rebuilt RS-3's fresh from Morrison-Knudson with 2000 HP 251-prime movers.

Whitehall, New York is just over the border from Rutland, Vermont and is a crew change and classification point for locals and through traffic to Rouses Point. The Sharks roll northbound past the station for Rouses Point in March 1975. *(Both photos, Jim Shaughnessy)*

With five GE U-23B's in their original numbers (now 2300 series), WR-1 rolls through Schenectady, New York. *(Jim Shaughnessy)*

For years, the Boston & Maine operated the "Selkirk Transfer" from Mechanicville west to Rotterdam Jct., then east on the New York Central West Shore line to Selkirk Yard. Now through B&M-PC pool runs are operated but on May 3, 1969, maroon GP-7's 1576-1574 bring M-1 through Hoffmans, New York. *(Jack Armstrong)*

XO Tower at the south end on Mechanicville Yard controls movements for both B&M and D&H. Jim Shaughnessy used the tower to frame shiny new GP-9 1700 arriving from Boston.

Rarely found on the B&M's west end during any period of their operation, Alco road switchers at Mechanicville in the late 1950's were good subject matter. *(Jim Shaughnessy)*

A pair of GP-7's crest the Mechanicville Hump in November 1975. Through the faded maroon paint on the short hood of the 1567 can be seen a Mannix Construction Co. emblem, reminder that this unit was leased to that company for track construction several years ago.

With tonnage from New England in tow, a trio of Lehigh Valley C-628's lift D&H train PB-99 out of Mechanicville on the joint D&H-B&M track between Mechanicville and Crescent. *(Both photos, George Melvin)*

GP-9's and GP-18's dominated the B & M's Mechanicville line for better than a decade. 1700's cross the Hoosick River near Valley Falls, New York.

The exceptions were notable...RS-3 1542 and RS-2 1532 roll eastbound into Valley Falls. *(Both photos - Jim Shaughnessy)*

Bennington local M-4 rolls over the Walloomsac River at North Hoosick, New York returning to Mechanicville from the Vermont Railway connection. *(Jim Shaughnessy)*

Two Penn Central GP-40's and a GP-35 are about to enter State Line Tunnel at Canaan, New York with an eastbound TV train for Boston. *(Jack Armstrong)*

Nearly airborne, a New Haven freight crosses the huge Hudson River bridge at Poughkeepsie, New York in 1961. *(D. A. Woodworth, Jr.)*

A quartet of New Haven GP-9's idle past a quartet of Ontario & Western FT's at the Maybrook engine terminal. *(Ontario & Western Technical & Historical Society)*

With a through run to Chicago, the Erie made good connections at Maybrook for New England traffic off the New Haven. Westbound BX-91 has 97 cars behind its two year old set of F-3's at Maybrook in 1949. *(Harold K. Vollrath Collection)*

Once rostering only RS-3's, the Lehigh & Hudson River bought the first C-420's in 1963. A trio of RS-3's leave Maybrook in 1964 with cars for the Pennsy and Reading. Penn Central takeover of the New Haven left the L&HR with a bridge road serving the PC at both ends. Traffic dwindled and the L&HR is going into ConRail in 1976. *(Neil Shankweiler)*

Lehigh & New England FA-1's cross the Erie diamonds at Campbell Hall, near Maybrook on June 15, 1961 just before the LNE was abandoned. *(Jack Swanberg)*

Railfan-favorite, the "hard-luck" Ontario & Western: FT's never looked better than this set arriving at Maybrook in 1950. *(George Melvin Collection)*

New Haven's group of ten 1200 HP Lima switchers were frequently assigned to Maybrook yard as is unit 637 in May, 1955. *(470 Club Collection)*

Grimy FL-9 5027 does work train duty with a wire train at Mamaroneck, New York in the Fall of 1972. *(Jerome A. Rosenfeld)*

AN ALBUM
OF "EXTRAS"

Much is written about the glamorous passenger trains, the fast freights and heavy mainline action. But what of the lowly "extras"? Although sometimes unnoticed in passing, there is an appealing nature about them. So, as a tribute, here is a collection of work trains, branchline mixed trains, helper engines and plow "extras."

A seldom seen, but versatile piece of equipment is the Jordan Spreader. Here is one in action on the Maine Central "Lower Road" mainline east of Richmond, Maine on June 22, 1963. GP-7 #567 provides enough push needed for the ditching job. *(George Melvin)*

A sad task! Claremont & Concord 13 heads up the scrap train near Contoocook, N. H. on the Emerson Branch in 1963. In the process of being pulled up, is the former Boston & Maine through line from Peterboro and Hillsboro. *(Walker Transportation Collection-Beverly Historical Society)*

New Haven GP-9 #1220 has an easy time as it rattles along with a crane in tow near Route 128 outside of Boston. *(Jay Potter)*

220

Those Mixed Trains . . . . .

Although Bangor & Aroostook's daily mixed train for the East Millinocket branch frequently saw BL-2's and GP-7's, occasionally the services of an NW-2 or F-3 were required. Here, above, the 803 leads the ancient wooden combine, sporting roller bearing trucks, at Millinocket in 1951. In the winter of the same year, an ice-encrusted 505 and three reefers prepare to leave town. *(Russ Munroe, Jr.)*

Boston & Maine's local mixed train from Manchester approaches the outskirts of Portsmouth, N. H. in this 1957 scene. *(Russ Munroe, Jr.)*

Canadian Pacific's Train 517 "The Scoot" ran well into the 1960's and a caboose as well as the combine was a usual part of the consist. While RS-18 8745 switches out pulpwood cars at Jackman, Maine in January 1963, the combine is spotted by the station. *(George Melvin)*

"Nope! . . . She's not takin' on water." Maine Central Mixed Train #378 has arrived at Groveton, N. H. over Boston & Maine trackage and SW-7 #332 prepares to place the combine on the other end. The reverse move is required in order for the train to head north over the Grand Trunk to North Stratford. *(Philip R. Hastings)*

Venerable combine brings up the rear of St. J. & L. C. Train #74 eastbound at Greensboro, Vermont. *(W. G. Fancher photo—Walker Transportation Collection of Beverly Historical Society)*

The Mountain Climbers

Maine Central F-3 units #683 and 682 and veteran URSA Mike #626 back downgrade over Frankenstein Trestle after pushing the first section of freight #376 to the summit of Crawford Notch, New Hampshire in February 1950. *(Philip R. Hastings)*

A show of power! Russ Munroe, Jr. provides us with a couple of views of a battle with gravity and friction on the 2.75% grade through Crawford Notch, N.H. on February 6, 1966. Westbound freight RY-2 is slowed to a crawl as it crosses Frankenstein Trestle with F-3 #684, GP-7's #569 and 572, and F-3 #672B and 672A up front.

At Notchland, below, about 100 plus cars to the rear, GP-7's #571 and 577 shove hard on the buggy to keep the slack bunched.

Boston & Maine's westbound Portland-Mechanicville freight gets a push by a pair of RS-2's (1531-1532) near Wachusett, Mass. on the Fitchburg Division on June 24, 1951. There are ruling grades in both directions on this line with helper engines assigned at Fitchburg and East Deerfield. *(Stan Bolton photo—Collection of Dave Albert)*

Almost obscured by the falling snow, an SD-45 shoves a freight over Washington grade near Dalton, Mass. on the old Boston & Albany line in February 1973. *(Jack Armstrong)*

SNOW COUNTRY! The white stuff is one of the major operating problems of the region's railroads. Just how severe "old man winter" can be is readily seen here, above, as Bangor & Aroostook's freight Extra 44 North, with plow up front, arrives Millinocket, Maine in February 1966 after an epic 75 mile, 12 hour battle with the elements. *(George Melvin)*

A Maine Central plow extra, below, rolls out of Waterville yard pass Tower "A" on January 3, 1969. Alco S-3 #961, sandwiched between Plow 82 and Jordan Spreader 799 will work west on the "Back Road" mainline to Leeds Junction and then clear the Rumford and Farmington branches; a long three day task. *(Dave Albert)*

Grand Trunk plow train rushes downgrade in a cloud of white at Berlin, New Hampshire in December 1968 as it clears the line east to Portland. *(J. Emmons Lancaster photo—Dwight A. Smith collection)*

Springfield Terminal #1, below, works the plow along the street trackage in Springfield, Vermont on December 27, 1966. The home-made combination plow, spreader, weed sprayer is winging back the snow on the left side of the track. *(Donald S. Robinson)*

George R. Cockle

EPILOGUE

As we have traced the diesel years of New England's railroads through the past four and a half decades, many changes have taken place with some periods being more active than others, and this brings to mind, as we ponder the years ahead: "Will there be as many changes in the future?"

The Nation's Bicentennial celebration and the railroads' participation in the festivities with colorful red, white, and blue locomotives, the increased activities of Amtrak in improving passenger service, and new concepts in motive power and equipment have brought the nation's railroads back into the public eye. In the Northeast, Conrail is now a reality and a New England merger looms on the distant horizon. As in the past, we can be assured that New England's railroads will be in the forefront of future developments in the industry.

So, it would appear that the answer to the above question would be a hearty "YES!!!!"

Dave Albert

NEW ENGLAND DIESELS